BE BOLD | BE TRANSPARENT | BE MORE

THE JOURNEY TO A NEW YOU

RAHUL THAKUR

First Published in December 2021

ISBN: 978-93-5472-373-5

BLUEROSE PUBLISHERS

www.bluerosepublishers.com

info@bluerosepublishers.com

+91 8882 898 898

Cover Design:

Aveek

Typographic Design:

Ilma Mirza

Distributed by: BlueRose, Amazon, Flipkart

THE JOURNEY TO A NEW YOU

Wow!! Finally, this is not your first book *Journey*

"I am not very intelligent, but I love intelligence
I am not a great person, but I love greatness."

अनारम्भस्तुकार्याणांप्रथमंबुद्धिलक्षणम्।
आरब्धस्यान्तगमनंद्वितीयंबुद्धिलक्षणम्॥

कार्य शुरु करना बुद्धि का पहला लक्षण है।
शुरु किये हुए कार्य को समाप्त करना बुद्धि का दूसरा लक्षण है।

Starting tasks is the first characteristic of intelligence. Once started,
bringing tasks to completion is the second characteristic of intelligence…

I am just INFINITELY fascinated by the magical process of LEARNING

This book is a tribute to ourselves, you will get to know why as you sail through...

I commit 10% of the royalty from the book to be dedicated to the heroes of the pandemic & another 10% for Afghan Relief for providing whatever little support I can, in mark of the respect to heroes who have shown character and fought. I urge this amount to be used in healthcare sector as well for providing support to the Afghan Refugees by the government.

I commit 20% of the royalty of the book to be dedicated to the slum kids that I take care. The amount will be used for the upkeep of their education, food & clothes.

Loading...

Dedicated to

"HUMANS AND THEIR EXCEPTIONAL ABILITIES"

One Machine can do the work of fifty ordinary humans, no machine can do the work of on extraordinary human

\- **Elbert Hubbard**

PREFACE

HOW THIS *JOURNEY* WILL BENEFIT YOU?

Do you like to `*feel better*` or `*get better*`?

While there is no problem in `*feel better*`, it is short lived and `*outside in*` that means external factors are responsible for change. Do you really want to give the control to external factors? Think about it! Motivational videos or songs or maybe even a book and speech can certainly make you `*feel better*`. But that is not a matter of interest for me as those tools are very rare and hardly help you to `*get better*`.

I am of the genre `*get better*` *where my locus of focus is to help you including myself to* `*get better*` rather than` *feel better*`. The reason is obvious as it has ever lasting impression and is driven by `*inside out*` methodology. Here you will have the responsibility and you will own your actions and thought process rather than the external ones which is dynamic and beyond our control.

This book or rather an extraordinary *voyage,* is tailor-crafted for you. It`s not about me and my experience; it is all about you; you are the hero of the book. More than a book, it's an expedition that you decide to sail through.

After you complete this journey, your personal expedition shall start towards exploring your possibilities. Believe me, **YOU are limitless.** The moment you realize this fact you will be a "New You" and start exploring yourself. I would recommend to not hustle and hurry up in reading, but rather to enjoy it along the ride exploring infinite possibilities. This is a hands-on practical scripture, where each section would call for action. Look for your 'ahaaa...' moments as you move gradually and practice along the way.

THE BEST WAY TO READ THIS BOOK

After each section/chapter, with your 'ahaaa...' call to action moment, ensure that you practice it for few days, let us say a week. Write down the differences that you observe with the new approach as compared to how you earlier behaved in the same situation. Make sure you are able to observe significant differences. And if this is not happening, the entire purpose of my writing this book is impractical.

Until it helps you 'get better', I will not consider this book as successful. I have attached a tool for you to help achieve this task. You can download, print and start documenting the progress that you are experiencing. I would personally suggest downloading it if you are serious for re-inventing yourselves and amend your ways.

And in any case if it does or it doesn't, you can connect with me personally over social media platforms. You may also decide to meet me virtually or in person to discuss. I will be delighted to know your thoughts, challenges of life and the significant changes that you are able to make through this book.

I will be delighted to receive feedback from you whether as good or as areas of improvement. It will help me a lot to publish revised editions and also cover other topics that you would like me to cover.

Reach me @:

https://www.linkedin.com/company/the-journey-to-a-new-you

https://www.facebook.com/simpliiawesome

https://www.instagram.com/rahul.thakurkp/

FOREWARD

This book is written with the intention to help you
`GET BETTER`

SO WHAT DO YOU UNPACK WITH *'THE JOURNEY TO A NEW YOU'*

1. Historical Present of the Future
2. Learning Optimization
3. Sports Psychology: Getting inside a Champion`s Mind.
4. Relationship with Technology
5. Dealing with the dares of Modern World
6. Understand how your brain functions 'In detail'
7. Exponentially Increased Mind Utilization
8. Increased Productivity & Efficiency
9. Significant Surge in Your Intelligence
10. Smart Dealing with Humans
11. Increased Self-Reflection, Self-Regulation, Self-Management, and Self-control
12. Fresh Perspective towards Life
13. Effective Professional Skills that make you stand out
14. Getting into self-motivated mode
15. Still looking for more...?

Ab bache ki jaan loge kya aap, kaafi nahi hai itna, hain?☺ !!! (Would you take this kiddo`s life? Aren't these enough☺!!

Just Kidding!! I don't want you to be very serious when you are sailing through the Trip. I will urge you to enjoy it just like you enjoy any delightful movie or a *zabardast (Amazing)* dish. For things we enjoy, our brain is receptive just like when your spouse`s mood is good, you will not be denied a lovely dress as a gift if you are a female and for the male counterparts, you may ask for a good cooked meal and something more...

After you complete reading this book, you will get a big-big surprise!! Would you like to know what that is? Ok no problem let me tell you. So the surprise that you are going to get is...Oh wait! Isn't surprise meant to be a surprise? I am Right or am I right?

Although, you can check your surprise right away mentioned at the last page of the book. Before you hover over the ending pages, may I ask you to not check now?

So now your mind pops the question as to "Why can`t I check now?" Am I Correct?
Let me answer that for you. I am not that bad to keep you dangling in dilemma.

The objective: ***To practice Self-control & Self-regulation.*** When you allow things to unfold at their own pace, at the right time, you enjoy every bit of it. We must learn to trust nature that eventually, everything, every problem will find its way to a solution. As a matter of fact none of the locks are manufactured without keys, so are the problems of life. We just need to adopt the right approach. And the right approach is to self-reflect, self-regulate and self-control. So why not start practicing it right away by not going to the last page to check what the surprise is. And when you are cruising through the Trip, your brain may pop up several times to go and peek in but remember self-control. This is how I am going to make you practice most of the things, as the journey of this bookunfolds.

So let us all check up from the neck up!

WHY YOU SHOULD OR SHOULDN'T SAIL THROUGH THIS *JOURNEY*

If you find a yes to any, some or all of the questions, then I promise you will thank yourself for deciding to start the expedition.

1. Do you want to re-invent yourself and wish to have a brand new 'You'?
2. Do you want to find the code to an efficient mind?
3. Were you *taught* what to learn and not *how* to learn?
4. Do you struggle to learn in school, college & profession?
5. Do you think crisis is an indication of something great?
6. Do you think COVID-19 has changed the world for better?
7. Do you think we should mend our ways of interacting with mother Earth?
8. Do you want to own yourself and time?

WHY AM I IN PURSUIT OF WRITING A BOOK?

The reason is straightforward and resonates with my life`s objective.

"I am passionate about impacting lives around me." It is the sole reason to hunt this challenging path. It gives me the kick, the motivation, the resources, and what not; to chase it. So, beholding my passion, I picked rare media that I am sure will help us both to accomplish our cravings together. For me, the primary ones are:

1. **Book Writing -** Self Development, Education, and others.
2. **TEDx Workshops:** Although, I still aspire to reach that stage. Waiting patiently for the big moment to share my knowledge on an international platform.
3. **Social Work -** Education, Healthcare, Women Empowerment, Child & Family, Old Age/ Disabled, Community Social Work, Public Policy Social Work.
4. **Training Workshops -** Training for Corporates, Educational Institutions, Slums, Jails and Transgender Society.
5. **Education Adoption -** Adopting a child`s education by providing requisite teaching and a conducive environment along with the resources to pursue education.

HOW AND WHY I WROTE THIS *JOURNEY*?

I wrote this book with the help of my fingers and a laptop!

Jokes apart! ☺

I arrived at the ways above through *Experiential & Transformative Learning*. I am fascinated by learning through my failures, successes, student & corporate lives, sports, music, traveling, powerful & effective conversations with real-life heroes & also successful personalities.

I concluded that there is so much *NOISE* ubiquitously. *THE JOURNEY TO A NEW YOU* presents the problems above with solutions to `get better` rather than `feel better`. The Prime reason for the *NOISE* is *DIGITAL DEMENTIA*, besides others. Additionally, there is a deficiency of motivation to pursue dreams. Don't you think that motivation is overrated? And even if it is available, it is not in abundance. Absence of *VALUES* in living lives. Helping others has become a thing of the past & it resonates with anxiety nowadays.

Nonexistence of resilience in dealing with failures. Existence of blurred goals. Skills that are ignored but are fundamental for our survival. The recent fresh spell of the Covid-19 Pandemic and Afghanistan Chaos has reinforced the need for must have skills.

A few of them are self-reflection, self-regulation, communication skills, problem-solving, critical thinking, comprehending, creativity, people management, emotional intelligence, resilience, motivation, focus, learning how to learn effectively, and the relationship with technology. Dealing with physical & mental health is also a growing concern, and has become much important than ever before.

And the good news!!! All the mentioned life skills are learnable as well as trainable. The better news is, the solution is in your hand right now. And the best news, I have tried to transmit these skills to you as much as possible so that you can take it upwards and onwards from here.

ALRIGHT, IT IS TIME THAT WE FASTEN OUR SEAT BEALTS NOW OR *SET OURSELVES FREE*

This very first chapter of the book is so apt to justify its title, ***"The Journey to a New You."*** The flight of a crisis has led us to get an ***insurance against failure – by Re-Inventing ourselves and our ways***. Moreover, it has led to a ***New Us*** by forcing to revisit the good old ways and to curb the path that we had unknowingly adopted.

First and foremost, I really appreciate the efforts that the brainy humans have put in to gift us the wonderful lives that we are experiencing today. You have made our lives easier with the kind of technology and innovations you have introduced, which has enabled us to pursue higher goals and deal our everyday challenges with much more ease and efficiency than ever before. Be it a primitive or an advanced one. Simplistic or complex, it helps us. Among the great ones, I have tried to give you a preview of some, which have always amazed me. These are just superb!

1. **Mother Nature: *The Only Perfect thing in the world.***
   All the other things are bound to be imperfect and have areas of improvement. But, it just amazes me to realize how perfect it is. And I really don't know whom to thank for this invention. Can you help me to identify please?

2. **WE, The Human Beings.**
   For every astounding invention that has come across, emanated after this invention. And all the inventions

whether they have a huge or bleak impact on the world has been through humans. So don't you think that humans should get their due credit? I leave this for you to answer.

https://interestingengineering.com/35-inventions-that-changed-the-world

3. Smart Bike:

On a recent trip to Chennai in September 2021, I was fascinated and amazed with the kind of technology we are experiencing. I am talking about smart bikes. While on a normal stroll after my lunch, I was with one of my colleagues, when I encountered as what is called as Smart Bike. We downloaded the app and scanned the QR code pasted on the bicycle and whoooohooo. It was unlocked with such a nominal fare.

My colleague and I, were so excited that we planned to go to the Marina Beach in Chennai about 6 to 7 Kms away from our office premises. We paddled our way to the fantastic beach in the evening. All the way through the road I was wondering about the bigger picture benefits besides other benefits of using this facility, which I have enumerated below:

a. Health Benefits
b. Pollution Control
c. Economic benefits
d. Reduction of traffic

Perhaps a small idea has the potential to bring long-lasting impact.

https://play.google.com/store/apps/details?id=production.smartbikemobility.customer&hl=en_IN&gl=US

Bicycles are a desirable form of transportation for many reasons, including the fact that taking a bicycle is environment-friendly, economically cost-effective, a way to stay fit and healthy and on occasions, an enjoyable social activity. In the post-pandemic scenario bicycles are acknowledged as the safest means of commuting. Bike-sharing, or public bicycle programs, have received increasing attention in recent years with initiatives to increase cycle usage, improve the first mile/last mile connection to other modes of transit, and lessen the environmental impacts of our transport activities.

SmartBike, a company run by passionate cyclists and entrepreneurs is India's largest Public Bicycle Sharing System Company in India and is operating world-class PBS systems in New Delhi, Chennai, Hyderabad & Chandigarh and soon in other cities. It has transformed the way bicycles are used on a sharing basis by the common citizens by providing high-quality bicycles at densely populated residential and commercial centers through the installation of bicycle stations.

The process of rent and return is digital and can be done on a smart phone. Riders can easily rent and return through our App from any SmartBike station and return at any SmartBike station in the city. SmartBike App is very user-friendly as it shows the nearest bike the station, number of bikes available at the station, the route to reach nearest bike station and captures all the post-ride details like distance traveled, calories burnt etc. SmartBike uses state of the art Smart bicycles, which are custom designed for Indian roads and fitted with a secure lock system. Each bicycle is integrated with SmartBike App which gives the rider, better access, and convenience to ride it. The bicycles can be rented from any SmartBike station and returned anywhere else at our stations within your city.

4. Films

My favorite film is "Barsaat". A romantic Bollywood comedy starring Bobby Deol & Twinkle Khanna, which one is yours? And yes "Lagaan" too featuring Aamir Khan, the perfectionist. Before I forget I will mention two more.. One would be "Chichhore" a Bollywood inspirational movie featuring late Sushant Singh Rajput who inspired millions. The way he perished left me speechless for few days. The flick teaches us "how to deal with failure".

https://en.wikipedia.org/wiki/Bhaag_Milkha_Bhaag

And the second one of my favorite list is "Bhaag Milkha Bhaag" a 2013 Hindi-language biographical sports drama film directed by Rakeysh Omprakash Mehra from a script written by Prasoon Joshi. The story is based on the life of Milkha Singh, an Indian athlete and Olympian who was a champion of the Commonwealth Games and two-times 400m champion of the Asian Games. It stars Farhan Akhtar in the titular role, with Sonam Kapoor, Divya Dutta, Meesha Shafi, Pavan Malhotra, Yograj Singh, Art Malik, and Prakash Raj in supporting roles. Sports was coordinated by the American action director Rob Miller of ReelSports.

Farhan Akhtar, a great actor I must say. I still remember the scene vividly wherein he shrieks for 2 to 3 minutes after returning to home when becoming successful and when he gifts his mom a new gold earring, for, his mom had sold the old ones to help him pursue his higher goals.

Almost every one of you love to watch movies and I bet you can`t deny the fact. In fact, I love to watch movies of various genres like a romance, comedy, drama, horror, suspense, action, fiction, biography, etc. A film is also called a movie, motion picture, theatrical film, photoplay, and flick. The name "film" originates from the fact that a photographic film has been the medium for recording and displaying motion pictures. Early inspirations for movies were the plays and dances, which had elements common to film: scripts, sets, costumes, production, direction, actors, audiences, and storyboards.

Later in the 17th century, the lanterns were used to project animation, which was achieved by various types of mechanical slides. In March 1895, the first motion picture film shot with a Cinématographe camera was La Sortie de leucine Lumière a Lyon (Workers leaving the Lumière factory at Lyon). The commercial, public screening of ten of Lumière brothers' short films in Paris on 28 December 1895 is often thought of as the start of projected cinematographic motion pictures.

With time, the movies have evolved to include sound, color, and advanced digital technology.

5. Petrol

Don't worry I don't want to highlight and discuss about the rocketing prices. I may love to discuss the alternatives though. Without gasoline, there would be no transportation industry as we know it today.

Gasoline is a fuel derivative of petroleum. It is called "gas" in the United States and "petrol" in other places around the world. To be more specific, petrol is a transparent, petroleum-derived liquid that is used as a fuel in internal combustion engines. Interestingly gas was initially discarded as an unwanted byproduct.

Before the discovery and commercialization of gasoline, the fuel of choice was a blend of alcohol, usually methanol, and turpentine called camphene, and later this would be largely replaced by kerosene. The first oil well dug in the US, in 1859, in Pennsylvania, refined the oil to produce kerosene. Although the distillation process also produced gasoline, this was discarded as a byproduct. The method of distillation refining only produced about 20 percent gasoline from a given amount of crude petroleum.

However, once it was discovered that the internal combustion engine ran best on light fuels like gasoline; the refining process was, well refined. In 1913, gasoline was produced more easily using chemical catalysts and pressure. The new thermal cracking process doubled the efficiency of refining and made refining gasoline more practical.

6. Battery Electricity & Battery

Perhaps the best alternative for petrol or at least as it is thought and the world is trying to conquer this domain for the better. Battery electricity has become the basic need for our day to day life, another essential invention. Of course, electricity itself has been here around all along, but the practical applications to effectively use it were invented later. Although many use electricity, how many of you know the history of electricity?

Alessandro Volta is generally credited with discovering the first practical battery. He invented his battery in 1799; it consisted of discs of two different metals, such as copper and zinc, separated by cardboard soaked in brine. In 1831, British scientist Michael Faraday discovered the basic principles of electricity generation. The electromagnetic induction discovery revolutionized energy usage. Street lights were some of the earliest attention gaining equipment. With the rise in electricity usability, now it stands as a backbone of modern industrial society.

The prehistoric battery may date back to the Parthian empire, which is around 2,000 years old. The ancient battery consisted of a clay jar filled with a vinegar solution, into which an iron rod surrounded by a copper cylinder was inserted.

These batteries might have been used to electroplate silver. But, as mentioned in the previous entry, the inventor of the first electric battery is Alessandro Volta, who developed the pile battery. After that, in 1802, William Cruickshank invented the Trough battery, an improvement on Alessandro Volta's voltaic pile.

Batteries had a breakthrough in 1859, with the invention of the first rechargeable battery based on lead-acid by the French physician Gaston Planté. The Nickel-Cadmium (NiCd) battery was introduced in 1899 by Waldemar Jungner. Did you know that new sodium-ion batteries could pave the way for sustainable battery production?

7. **Antibiotics**

Perhaps Covid-19 has been something new for us but not Antibiotics. They havesaved millions of lives by killing and inhibiting the growth of harmful bacteria. Louis Pasteur and Robert Koch first described the use of antibiotic drugs in 1877. In 1928, Alexander Fleming identified penicillin, which is derived from mold. Throughout the 20th century, antibiotics spread rapidly and proved to be a major living improvement, fighting nearly every known form of infection and protecting peoples' health.

8. **Contraceptives**

Prevention of pregnancy has a long and determined history. The history of contraceptives dates back at least to 1500 B.C, where records indicate that ancient Egyptian women would mix honey, sodium carbonate, and crocodile dung into a thick, solid paste called pessary and insert it into their reproductive organs before intercourse. However, many researchers believe that old world birth control methods like these are not effective, and indeed, possibly life threatening.

The first known form of condom (a goat bladder) was used in Egypt around 3000 B.C. In 1844 Charles Goodyear patented the vulcanization of rubber, which led to the mass production of rubber condoms. In 1914 with a monthly newsletter called "The Woman Rebel", Margaret Sanger, a great female educator from New York State, first coined the term "Birth control." Later, Carl Djerassi had successfully created a progesterone pill, which could block ovulation.

The Pill launched an international revolution that allowed women to determine when they want to have children, and freed them from unplanned pregnancy, which could derail their careers and lives.

9. **The Refrigerator**

Do you remember the incident when stocks of Coca-Cola deep-dived, because, Cristiano Ronaldo, the football champ, preferred to have water instead of the cold-drink somewhere around June, 2021? It created a buzz all over the internet and that made me realize how powerful every single act of living legends can be.

Over the last 150 years, refrigeration has offered us ways to preserve food, medicines, and other perishable substances. Before its conception, people cooled their food with ice and snow. James Harrison built the first practical vapor compression refrigeration system. However, the first widespread refrigerator was the General Electric "Monitor-Top" refrigerator of 1927. While it helped to rev up industrial processes initially, it became an industry itself later on.

10. **Television**

My mom is behind me to get our television repaired and it has been almost a year that I have been trying to shy away. I think I may gift her a new television after getting published what you are currently reading. Depends on the sales though, hahhaha! You can help me to gift my mom a new television, indirectly though. Think about it!

In 2021, we can look for LED, LCD, or even curved display. Wow! Hats off to the imagination of human beings. Television! A small box with the ability to deliver such enormous amounts of information and has changed entertainment and communications forever. The invention of television was the work of many individuals. Although TV plays an important part in our everyday lives, it rapidly developed during the 19th and the 20th century as a result of the work of a number of people.

In 1884, a 23-year-old German university student, Paul Julius Gottlieb Nipkow patented the image rasterizer, a spinning disk with a spiral pattern of holes in it, so each hole scanned a line of an image. The first demonstration of the instantaneous transmission of images was by Georges Rignoux and A. Fournier in Paris in 1909. In 1911, Boris Rosing and his student Vladimir Zworykin created a system that used a mechanical mirror-drum scanner to transmit crude images over wires to a cathode ray tube or in a receiver. But the system was not sensitive enough to allow moving images.

In the 1920s, Scottish inventor John Logie Baird used the Nipkow disk to create a prototype video system. On March 25, 1925, Baird gave the first public demonstration of televised images in motion. On January 26, 1926, he demonstrated the transmission of an image of a face in motion using radio. This is widely regarded as being the world's first public television demonstration.

11. The Camera

Isn`t camera an important aspect our decision making process to purchase a stylish handset? Yes indeed but do you know some cool things about camera. It is undoubtedly one of the most cherished creations. This modern invention has witnessed many phases of evolution — camera obscura, daguerreotypes, dry plates, calotypes, SLRs, and DSLRs. In 1826, Joseph Nicéphore Niépce used a sliding wooden box camera made by Charles and Vincent Chevalier to click what is credited as the first permanent photograph.

With technological advancements, Digital cameras were introduced to save pictures on memory cards rather than using films. The history of the digital camera began with Eugene F. Lally's idea to take pictures of the planets and stars. Later, Kodak engineer Steven Sasson invented and built the first digital camera in 1975. It was built using parts of kits that were lying around the Kodak factory. The camera was about the size of a breadbox and it took 23 seconds to capture a single image. Today, every smart phone has at least one built-in camera that can also take videos.

You can freeze the great moments from your life in the form of photographs with better quality and superior handling digital camera. One doesn't have to look much further than a photo album to see that cameras are one of the great inventions that changed the world. Moreover, when I am writing this, I had put the battery for a DSLR on charge for shooting YouTube training videos for you. This camera, I could manage to borrow is a Nikon D5300 DSLR camera, from my friend Abhishek Gupta.

12. Telephone and Mobile Phones

"Hey!! Can we plan a meeting tomorrow?" Or "Mom, I may get late tonight as I have work in office," though you are at friend`s place with some cocktails, mock tails, delightful food and much more... At least I have done such conversation almost every week. Please don't let her know☺, or I should say that my mom is smart enough to suddenly ask – "Beta zara Video call krna, Kuch discuss krna hai". ("Son, make a video call, I need to discuss something"). What about your mom and dad? I would love to hear that from you and what excuses have you made to smartly get out of such situation. It will help me a lot for my stuff.

"Mr. Watson, come here, I want you." On March 10, 1876, these were the first words spoken by inventor of the telephone, Alexander Graham Bell, to his assistant Thomas Watson. Telephone history conceivably started with the human desire to communicate far and wide. With the arrival of the mobile phone in the 1980s, communications were no longer shackled to cables.

The clever invention of the cellular network supported the revolution of the telephone industry. Starting from bulky mobile phones to ultrathin handsets, mobile phones have covered a long way so far. John F. Mitchell and Martin Cooper of Motorola demonstrated the first handheld device in 1973. Scientists continue to create new ideas that will further help users.

13. Email

Let us imagine a situation where you don't have email in this world. How would you work then? What would be the tool you will choose to serve the purpose that email does? I would like to know from you.

I must say, without emails we are incomplete these days. Most developers of early mainframes and minicomputers developed similar, but often incompatible mail applications. Over time, these became linked by a web of gateways and routing systems. Many US universities were part of the ARPANET, which increased software portability between its systems. That portability helped make the

Simple Mail Transfer Protocol (SMTP) increasingly influential. The first ARPANET email was sent in 1971.

A man by the name of Ray Tomlinson is actually credited with inventing one common feature of the email system that we know today. In 1972, while working as an ARPANET contractor, Tomlinson chose to use the "@" symbol to denote the sending of messages from one computer to another computer. By the mid-1970s, email had taken on the form we recognize today. In the present-day, most of the official business communication depends on email.

14. Credit Cards

Alright, you get promotional telesales calls for Credit cards for which you get angry. At the dawn of the 20th century, most people paid for everything with cash.

The idea of the credit card was introduced around 1950 by Ralph Schneider and Frank McNamara, the founders of Diners Club, which allowed diners to sign for their meal and then pay later. While the technology continues to advance, the idea of paying for daily purchases with credit has now become the norm.

15. ATM

Taking it further to the saying that cash is king, the invention of the ATM (Automated Teller Machine) is very important to modern banking. According to the ATM Industry Association (ATMIA), there are now over 2.2 million ATM machines installed worldwide. Many experts believe that the first ATM was the creation of Luther Simjian, called Bankograph.

In 1967, John Shepherd-Barron led the team that came up with a bright idea of a money vending machine, which was implemented by a London bank called Barclays. These machines used single-use tokens which had been impregnated with radioactive carbon-14. The radioactive signal was detected by the machine and matched against a personal identification number entered on a keypad. Soon, rival cash dispenser systems began to emerge, including one that used a reusable plastic card instead of a radioactive token. Dallas Engineer Donald Wetzel devised the first automated banking machine in the U.S.

16. Guns

I still have 2 guns in my cupboard right now when I am writing this without license none of the police stations know it. I urge you all too, to please keep it a secret as I have a deep fascination for guns since my childhood, though the toy ones!

For some, guns might be a sensational invention while for others it might be a dreadful one. Weapons have been used since the dawn of humanity. But it is an undeniable fact that guns and gunpowder had revolutionized the world. Gunpowder was invented in China in around the 9th century, but it may have initially been used for fireworks. One early firearm consisted of a bamboo tube that used gunpowder to fire a spear, and was used in China around 1000 AD.

Another early type of portable firearm was the fire lance, a black-powder–filled tube attached to the end of a spear and used as a flamethrower; shrapnel was sometimes placed in the barrel so that it would fly out together with the flames. A fire-lance is depicted on a mid-10th century silk banner from China.

Gunpowder was made more powerful by increasing the amount of saltpeter. This, in turn, meant that a stronger barrel was needed, and the bamboo was replaced by metal, and the projectiles were replaced by smaller pieces of metal that fit into the barrel more tightly. By the mid-to-late 14th century, knowledge of gunpowder and firearms had reached Europe and smaller, portable hand-held cannons were developed, creating a type of personal firearm.

The problem of needing to reload frequently was solved with the invention of a hand-driven machine gun called the Gattling gun. It was invented by Richard J. Gatling during the American Civil War. As the tech has continued to evolve, each following model has become deadlier.

https://en.wikipedia.org/wiki/Artificial_intelligence

17. Artificial Intelligence

Which web-series did you recently complete watching on Netflix? Was it "The Family Man" or Pataal Lok? Or maybe you choose a different platform altogether. Did you choose Amazon Prime for that matter? I will tell you mine. I recently completed watching SUITS. It was the only escape that I gave myself while finishing up the 'thing' that you are reading now. I must admit that I haven't used Netflix or Amazon Prime yet. I viewed the web-series on YouTube. And before I forget to mention, I am sure you have been hearing a lot about Alexa and Siri.

Do you know how such platforms recognize what you would like to see next and they give you recommendations? It is interesting though to know the magic behind it. Quite intelligent these platforms are, right?

This is where artificial intelligence comes in. And how do I know? Trust me, I will not mislead you. I recently completed my Masters in Data Science from Purdue University, where I was fascinated by the kind of role Artificial Intelligence is playing.

Artificial intelligence (AI) is intelligence demonstrated by machines, as opposed to the natural intelligence displayed by humans or animals. Leading AI textbooks define the field as the study of "intelligent agents": any system that perceives its environment and takes actions that maximize its chance of achieving its goals. Some popular accounts use the term "artificial intelligence" to describe machines that mimic "cognitive" functions that humans associate with the human mind, such as "learning" and "problem solving"

AI applications include advanced web search engines, recommendation systems (used by YouTube, Amazon and Netflix), understanding human speech (such as Siri or Alexa), self-driving cars (e.g. Tesla), and competing at the highest level in strategic game systems (such as chess and Go).There are much more that can be added to the list.

Artificial intelligence was founded as an academic discipline in 1956, and in the years since has experienced several waves of optimism, followed by disappointment and the loss of funding (known as an "AI winter"), followed by new approaches, success and renewed funding. AI research has tried and discarded many different approaches during its lifetime, including simulating the brain, modeling human problem solving, formal logic, large databases of knowledge and imitating animal behavior. In the first decades of the 21st century, highly mathematical statistical machine learning has dominated the field, and this technique has proved highly successful, helping to solve many challenging problems throughout industry and academia.

The various sub-fields of AI research are centered on particular goals and the use of particular tools. The traditional goals of AI research include reasoning, knowledge representation, planning, learning, natural language processing, perception and the ability to move and manipulate objects. General intelligence (the ability to solve an arbitrary problem) is among the field's long-term goals. To solve these problems, AI researchers use versions of search and mathematical optimization, formal logic, artificial neural networks, and methods based on statistics, probability and economics. AI also draws upon computer science, psychology, linguistics, philosophy, and many other fields.

The field was founded on the assumption that human intelligence "can be so precisely described that a machine can be made to simulate it". This raises philosophical arguments about the mind and the ethics of creating artificial beings endowed with human-like intelligence. These issues have been explored by myth, fiction and philosophy since antiquity. Some people also consider AI to be a danger to humanity if it progresses unabated. Others believe that AI, unlike previous technological revolutions, will create a risk of mass unemployment.

Thought-capable artificial beings appeared as storytelling devices since bygonet, and have been common in fiction, as in Mary Shelley's Frankenstein or Karel Čapek's R.U.R. These characters and their fates raised many of the same issues now discussed in the ethics of artificial intelligence.

The study of mechanical or "formal" reasoning began with philosophers and mathematicians in history. The study of mathematical logic led directly to Alan Turing's theory of computation, which suggested that a machine, by shuffling symbols as simple as "0" and "1", could simulate any conceivable act of mathematical deduction. This insight, that digital computers can simulate any process of formal reasoning, is known as the Church–Turing thesis. Along with concurrent discoveries in neurobiology, information theory and cybernetics, this led researchers to consider the possibility of building an electronic brain. Turing proposed changing the question from whether a machine was intelligent, to "whether or not it is possible for machinery to show intelligent behavior". The first work that is now generally recognized as AI was McCullouch and Pitts' 1943 formal design for Turing-complete "artificial neurons".

The field of AI research was born at a workshop at Dartmouth College in 1956, where the term "Artificial Intelligence" was coined by John McCarthy to distinguish the field from cybernetics and escape the influence of the cyberneticist Norbert Wiener. Attendees Allen Newell (CMU), Herbert Simon (CMU), John McCarthy (MIT), Marvin Minsky (MIT) and Arthur Samuel (IBM) became the founders and leaders of AI research. They and their students produced programs that the press described as "astonishing". Computers were learning checkers strategies, 1954, and by 1959 were reportedly playing better than the average human), solving word problems in algebra, proving logical theorems (Logic Theorist, first run c. 1956) and speaking English. By the middle of the 1960s, research in the U.S. was heavily funded by the Department of Defense and laboratories had been established around the world. AI's founders were optimistic about the future: Herbert Simon predicted, "Machines will be capable, within twenty years, of doing any work a man can do". Marvin Minsky agreed, writing, "Within a generation... the problem of creating 'artificial intelligence' will substantially be solved".

They failed to recognize the difficulty of some of the remaining tasks. Progress slowed and in 1974, in response to the criticism of Sir James Lighthill and ongoing pressure from the US Congress to fund more productive projects, both the U.S. and British governments cut off exploratory research in AI. The next few years would later be called an "AI winter", a period when obtaining funding for AI projects was difficult.

In the early 1980s, AI research was revived by the commercial success of expert systems, a form of AI program that simulated the knowledge and analytical skills of human experts. By 1985, the market for AI had reached over a billion dollars. At the same time, Japan's fifth generation computer project inspired the U.S and British governments to restore funding for academic research. However, beginning with the collapse of the Lisp Machine market in 1987, AI once again fell into disrepute, and a second, longer-lasting winter began.

AI gradually restored its reputation in the late 1990s and early 21st century by finding specific solutions to specific problems, such as logistics, data mining or medical diagnosis. By 2000, AI solutions were being widely used behind the scenes. The narrow focus allowed researchers to produce verifiable results, exploit more mathematical methods, and collaborate with other fields (such as statistics, economics and mathematics).

Faster computers, algorithmic improvements, and access to large amounts of data enabled advances in machine learning and perception; data-hungry deep learning methods started to dominate accuracy benchmarks around 2012. According to Bloomberg's Jack Clark, 2015 was a landmark year for artificial intelligence, with the number of software projects that use AI within Google increased from a "sporadic usage" in 2012 to more than 2,700 projects. Clark also presents factual data indicating the improvements of AI since 2012 supported by lower error rates in image processing tasks. He attributes this to an increase in affordable neural networks, due to a rise in cloud computing infrastructure and to an increase in research tools and datasets. In a 2017 survey, one in five companies reported they had "incorporated AI in some offerings or processes".

18. Machine learning

Machine learning (ML) is the study of computer algorithms that improve automatically through experience and by the use of data. It is seen as a part of artificial intelligence. Machine learning algorithms build a model based on sample data, known as "training data", in order to make predictions or decisions without being explicitly programmed to do so. Machine learning algorithms are used in a wide variety of applications, such as in medicine, email filtering, speech recognition, and computer vision, where it is difficult or unfeasible to develop conventional algorithms to perform the needed tasks.

So far so good, but in times of the disaster we felt helpless. The above mentioned inventions helped us a lot in combating the pandemic and still are doing. But somewhere, the need of the hour was to stop ***EVERYTHING***, and to be safe. Would it be wise to say that we had put ***an axe on our own foot*** with inventions and developments or was it the co-relationship with nature that caused a helpless situation? Again, this is a matter of debate. I would urge you to help me to navigate and figure out the relationship of nature with invention.

I leave that up to you to decide. It is very rightly said that ***NATURE FINDS ITS WAY***. I am still figuring out. It may be the aggressive expansion, rapid urbanization and the quality of interaction with Mother Nature.

So, the entire episode of the pandemic COVID`19 provided us with a new insight or rather made us to revisit the basics of life of good health, humanity, spending time at home with our loved ones. Nature yet again proved that humanity is the best religion that can ever exist. We must progress with time but not at the expense of interacting at such a level with our ***Mother Earth*** that it has to turn sideways to teach us a lesson. We will revisit the ride closely later in our trip, but this time with the ***intention to `get better` and teach ourselves as well as the upcoming generation*** of the moral ways of interacting with our planet and to curb the evil ways.

Have you ever wondered during the pandemic outbreak what the birds and animals across the world would have thought not seeing the usual hustle-and-bustle of humans? I still remember the scene on usual roads that I took, and let me be honest, that it was terrifying not to see a single individual along the streets. It resonated like a sci-fi Hollywood movie scene that shows the end of human civilization. I had never ever imagined seeing such an dystopian picture.

Anyways, the creatures could neither see traffic nor flying machines in the sky. Neither the roadside animals could see their better off counterparts living with the 'haves' of society coming out with belts around their neck.
I keep calling this book a journey rather than a book, and please bear with me for this. We will try to figure out the reason for asking this question together later in our expedition.

A lot of people ask me, aren't you afraid and fearful about the performance of the book. Aren't you worried? Now I refer these questions as *NOISE,* which you will come all across your passage. Let me tell you: Questions are compelling. They can make or break you.

So, whenever someone asks you a question, be careful about *what* and *how* you answer. It also resonates with the situation when you are on the other side of the table; I mean the time when you are in a position to ask questions.

My answer to the question of fear and other doubts is beyond suspicion. More than being fearful and doubtful, I am somewhat if not totally, immune to fear. As *Sattvic Gunas* dominate my thought process which I developed over the years derived from Shrimad Bhagvad Gita. I have also tried to give a glimpse of what you may learn from the holy book. I am as thrilled and excited as I was when I was to face a fast bowler in one of my cricket matches, who was ten years elder than me while I was just thirteen.

I am glad and thankful to the almighty for guiding me for the thought process of writing a ***journey***. You must have heard of *"Journey to the west."* Ours is going to be of a very different kind at the end of which you will find ***A NEW YOU & A NEW WORLD***. And in this ride with **the positive outlook of COVID19**, I am sure the rarest of the rare drive that we together with the world, will be sailed through. The best part, *we didn't need a vehicle for this trip.*

So, let us all meet ourselves at the end of the flight. This is *THE JOURNEY TO A NEW YOU.* You are the hero of the book and I will consider myself here as just a driver who is helping you to meet yourself. Sometimes, to meet ourselves, we have to go far. And the ticket price is sometimes slightly higher if you are late or *procrastinate*. So, choose to get an early bird discount or else be ready to pay a much higher price to meet yourself.

And let me ask you all, by the way, who makes the choices and decisions for you? Whether it's you or somebody else deciding for you, let us board through a beautiful flight, and I will be a trustworthy driver. But we must promise ourselves, that when we all reach our destinations, we will take a look back at the voyage-

It is not ultimately what you get; it is actually what you become while getting there.

So, whenever I get a book in my hand, I wonder, have I taken a good book? Or is it just another book in the market? Do you know why these questions pop-up in my mind?

It`s due to *DIGITAL DEMENTIA*, oh yes! Umm!! Figuring out, "Did I hear this term?" Oh yes! You certainly did a few lines before. I will nicely unpack this term later on in the upcoming sections. The best example of this term can be routed back to a day when on 3rd March 2020, India`s PM Shri Narendra Modi tweeted about leaving social media.

You are the owner of your decisions, and eve
n if you are not, I will make sure you become the one. You are free to go ahead and think, and those who are already onboard let us start.

For those who want to take time to think, we will be glad to meet you at some point in your incredible and unique personal trip, but still, we will welcome you and from there, you can come onboard, but the prices for the same ride would be slightly higher. So *early birds* enjoy a discount of enriched and exceptional experience.

And yes, before I forget to tell you that I am a people-oriented person, so whenever in this trip you come across terms like *fee, discount, waiver, compensation, price* and others, please be a little careful and patient as you have to look out for the actual meaning that I am referring to. Don't worry. I will make the real meanings of these words very easy to understand. So, the first ones where I used the term "prices" & "early bird discount" just a few lines before, could you figure out what kind of price the latecomers would have to pay and what do I mean by early bird discount?

Do you want me to help you here? Umm. No, not here. I will suggest you to try yourself first.

BOOK CHAPTERS

ACKNOWLEDGEMENT

आचार्यत्पादमादत्तेपादंशिष्यःस्वमेधया।
पादंसब्रह्मचारिभ्यःपादंकालक्रमेणच॥

अर्थात् (विद्यार्थीअपना एक-चौथाई ज्ञानअपने गुरु से प्राप्त करता है, एक चौथाई अपनी बुद्धि से प्राप्तकरता है, एक-चौथाई अपनेसहपाठियों से और एक-चौथाई समय के साथ (कालक्रम से, अनुभव से) प्राप्त करता है।

Meaning – A learner learns 1/4th of his knowledge from his teachers, 1/4th from his own mind, 1/4th from friends/colleagues and the remaining 1/4th from time.

Thank you Note:

While we are hustling in our lives confronting and conquering everyday challenges to pursue higher goals, it is very important to take a moment to appreciate what we have been blessed with. Real happiness is appreciating what/whom we get instead of getting what we like. And, also the contributions made by wonderful humans (the greatest invention of all time, for it to be, everything else followed after) that you could get a chance to meet in this amazing 'gift of life'. This wonderful Voyage couldn't be completed without the contributions of these human beings. If you have been good at keeping relationships and lucky at the same time the person will be with you always, forget about the distance.

Names are mentioned in chronological order of my life events. Just to mention that I have not taken the permission to use their names but still I have used them. To my dear `wonder humans` - "The only reason I didn't take permission is to give you all a surprise and to make you sense the emotion with which I have mentioned you as a contributor towards my life. Please bear with me for this". Although I have changed the names for most listed here.

"I want to say a sincere ***Thank You*** *for being a part of my life. I am just a reflection of the qualities that you have helped me to develop. Without you I couldn't have become the one I am today- A New ME"*

1. **Devi Ji**|My Sweetheart|10th October 2021 – Lifetime |*For giving a Promising head start to my life. If you wonder why I call you `Devi Ji`, just feel it, and you will be happy to embrace the answer. Ever since I have met you, the world seems much more beautiful it never seemed before, the sun even looks brighter, and the moon even more beautiful with your presence. Your aura is so enlightening and energizing that I get refreshed every time I see, think or feel about you. I know I may not be the perfect guy for you, but you are the one I have always wished for. Thank you for being a part of my life and accepting me and my family, though you tried your best not to get into marriage right away. Hahahahha. But you know what, my wish and prayer was much stronger to be together. Thank you for making my parents re-live their envisioned dream life. I wish you happiness as*

always and that notorious smile, the best make up that you put on. I cannot have dreamed of a better person than you. It's your presence that makes me complete. All the love and affection to you to the best of my ability and I promise I will keep you happy always and by the time you read this, you would have learned to drive four-wheeler with or without hitting anyone. Remember if you want to hit someone, hit from the rear side-- less damages to the car and you will be in better position to run away....

2. **Mr. Ishan Sai** |My dear friend| Don't exactly remember the Starting Point (I guess 1995 or even before that) but with me till date, my life`s first friend| *For being a true friend. Got to meet & reconnect with him after 17 years of separation. We disconnected as I was thrown out of a prestigious Institution for poor grades. I still possess and cherish the school group photo with him and our teachers-'Gurus'. He is the first person who gave me the qualities of 'being bold' and 'being more' apart from being courageous, he was an active participant in martial arts then. Currently handling printing press, his father`s business and taking care of family as a responsible son.*

3. **Mr. Sunny Singh & Family** |My dear friend-nicknamed as *'Lale di Jaan'*| 1995-Till date| *For being a true friend and implanting the spirit of sportsmanship and cricketing skills. He helped me to fill my vacant hours with productive hobbies of sketching & creative writing. "Lale di jaan, if you are reading this, you may recollect the story 'Band Darwaza' that we had written together- the very*

first creative and imaginative writing of our lives. We together can still complete it though! Currently, he is a Lawyer and supporting his family and his father in the court of law.

4. **Mrs. Sangeeta Sharma** |Principal & Director, A Prestigious Educational Institution in Jharkhand|2003-Till Date| *For believing and taking a risk for me despite knowing that I was so poor at studies when I met her. It was a life-changing event to meet and get her as my principal. If it didn't happen, I would have been no one. Her contributions in my life are beyond words. It was her, with whom I could become a studious student and a habit of reading was firstly instilled and established forever. Currently, she heads the same Prestigious Institution which has been developed largely. She still is developing and nurturing thousands like me and much better than me. The strongest and a lead by example lady whom I have ever known personally. The only time I saw her weak and crying was when she lost her grown up child way back around 2006. Recently, I saw an amazing rap sung and performed by our school students directed and ideated by Kuhu, her daughter. This rap amused me and my principal`s expression of anger in the video was quite natural. To get angry, she didn't need to act as anger is her jewelry. Those who can see the softness and care behind her anger are the lucky ones and fortunately I am among one of them.*

5. **Late Mr. Rajesh Kumar**|My dear friend|2004-2013| *For being my friend and trusting me. It was him who helped me sail through a never-ending struggle and kept me 'alive' with the medium of*

sports. Unfortunately, he is no more when I am writing this. "We miss you and soon I will visit your home to give you a surprising gift, hope you will like it."

6. **Mr. Suraj Kumar** |My dear friend|2004-Till date| *For being my friend and helping with studies. It was you who helped me to score marks and gradually I became one of the highest achievers. I was a complete zero in studies before meeting you.* Currently settled in UK, working as a support Engineer in IT sector with a Prominent Indian Brand.

7. **Aashna** |My dear friend|2006-till date| *For being a great friend and possessing a strong character, it was interesting to meet you after such a long time or to be more precise the first time in Kolkata unmarried, just few days away to know that you are getting married. You are a lucky one to get married to a person who loves you a lot. Thanks for accepting my unending friendship. I still remember the Raksha bandhan day somewhere around 2006, where I ran away from you in the fear of getting entangled in sister-brother relation. And the sweet that I made you eat that day as it was your birthday, was a big one..I know...but you ate it amazingly...*

8. **Mr. Vipul Kandoi & Family**|My dear friend and his family|2007| *For trusting me and helping me to survive with food and shelter during one of the weakest point and life-changing events of my lifetime.*

9. **Mr. Sushil Thakur**|My maternal grand-father|2007-Till date| *For taking care of my education, food, shelter, clothes and providing a conducive environment to study. Your contributions are speechless and I have no words to explain.*

10. **Late Ms. Ratna Dhar , Ms. Deepti Singh Karakoti, Mr. Sukanto Bhattacharya, Mr. Chanchal Roy Chowdhary, Ms. Purnima Das, Ms. Jayashree Acharya, Ms. Gargi Goswami** |2007-Till Date| *For believing in me. I was going through one of the weakest points of my life and it was because of you all that I could breathe and educate myself. The kind of culture that is fostered over the years in the school is priceless. It had been the most wonderful 2 years of my journey. I could see myself growing. It was because of your trust that I could develop public speaking skills, the school being the starting point. And to add-on, I found my first crush also…hahaha! She was beautiful indeed and Jayashree Mam, you may be reminded of the girl with whom you saw me talking for hours on an auspicious day. The crowd also helped me to learn a bit of healthy flirting.*

11. **Mr. Abhishek Gupta** |2007-Till Date|| *For being my `Janeman`, and the go to person. We failed together and succeeded seeing each other. I still remember the day when we cried for a four wheeler for our meeting with a beautiful girl for our project. Now I am sure your `dhanno` the car your brought and `sexy lady` - the one I possess now have become good friends. I was so upset the day uncle passed away despite our best efforts but you know what, he is there with you and seeing you*

succeed. Make a promise to your dad that you are going to rock the world and I am sure you will. You know that we are not ordinary performers. We are simply awesome! The only concern I have is when are we going to sit for the cold coffee again with such fullness and ease of life and observing things?? By the time you read this you know what, I am right now sitting at the same spot of cold-coffee place. The chair is empty but I can feel you-` friendship vala`, not the other one, that we are discussing our plans to be executed and this time we are not going to fail. The only options are to either win or learn.

12. **Mr. Ankit Verma** |2007-Till Date| *For preparing the lip-smacking `Allu Bonda` on my visits for night stay at your place. Interestingly I had decided to write about you at your seat in your room using your electricity and your bed. I will not ever say Sorry that I use your stuff too much but I just feel like using it. Thanks for being there in times of need. The day I came to hand over to you, four coconut when you were suffering from Covid, you didn't allow me to meet you. I cried and thought I would never be able to meet you or may be, I would lose you, the feeling itself was so scary, I can`t tell you I had to regain my strength to drive back to home. I had lost it when you denied me to meet you. My mind played that song that day "Jaane nahi denge tujhe" from 3 Idiots . By the time you would read this I guess, we both would be married at least to different girls or otherwise our marriage dates would even have clashed and the girls too. You know how much parallel and similar our life runs.*

13. **Mr Ravindra Arya** |My first Boss |2011-Till date| *For building my public speaking and presentation skills. It was you who trusted me and allowed me to expand and exercise my expertise.*

14. **Mr Sahil Khan** |My Boss|2016| *For being so humane and trusting me like his own younger brother. I also want to thank you for that 'Extra' pocket money apart from the salary that you paid. Also, a special mention of the opportunity that you allowed me to host the TV Show, that helped me groom myself for camera. It was till date the best project that I had handled. I still have it on my YouTube channel. It helped me a lot in tough times to take care of my family. The 'end' was not so good; perhaps it was not the end at all. It was a new beginning as you whispered in my ears. I still cherish that Hug that we shared when I left from the premises. I would surely love to work under your guidance once again.*

15. **Ms. Sonia Gahlot** |My Ex-Boss, and Assistant Vice-President, A top-notch MNC @ Gurgaon|2018-Till Date| *For being a good boss and a rude boss, sister, mother and a great friend. You are the best boss that I have ever got. I wish for your happiness and yes we are not going to put more weight from now onwards. I am sorry to trouble you a lot but you know what I love to trouble you and would love to trouble you again to work together. Hahahhah. With you some fine day. Only thing I need- Green Tea that you offered in the office, Mario and you.*

16. **Ms. Anchal Pandey** |'My special friend'|2018-2021| *For making me feel special, and bearing with me and all my anger, resentment, ignorance, hatred and the cold words that I have ever spoken. I am sorry and I can feel the pain that you have to go through due to my absurd and rude behavior. Time has taught me and 'karma' has played its role. You have treated me with such a trustworthiness and enthusiasm that no one has ever treated me. I can't thank you with words. I have never seen a girl of such a strong character and will power. I will always respect you, your honesty and contributions towards me and my parents.*

17. **Mr. Amit Raj** |My Current Boss, Head AGM-HR, Renowned Indo-Spanish MNC|2020-Till Date| *For hiring and trusting in my abilities. You have always supported me and provided me the liberty to work the way I wished and have been available in times of need. You have delivered me a very conducive environment so I could be the best version of myself and move upwards and onwards.*

18. **Mr Oscar Estebansanchez** |CEO, Renowned Indo-Spanish MNC|2020-Till Date| *For accepting me in the organization and being strict with constructive feedback highlighting precisely the errors that I had committed. It has helped me to polish myself and improve up to my best version. You as a leader possess such qualities that I look up to own one day!*

19. **Mr. Avinash Kumar** |President, Renowned Indo-Spanish MNC|2020-Till Date| *For being available for support and empathetic enough for me to trust and believe that I am at the right place and the right time. You have supported, encouraged, accepted new ideas and built the foundations strong as a leader. You possess humane qualities that I have always looked up to in a leader.*

20. **Maria Angeles Bosch** |HR-Director Asia-Oceania-Africa, Renowned Indo-Spanish MNC|2020-Till Date| *For understanding and allowing room for errors. It has helped me to re-affirm the belief that I have always gotten amazing women in my life. It truly and accurately resonates with the saying that "Behind every successful man, there is a Woman. And in my case I have been gifted with such Women in abundance. " You are an amazing person with fantastic approach to human relations.*

21. **Mr. Dinesh Gupta** |Executive Vice-President, Renowned Indo-Spanish MNC|2020-Till Date| *For questioning and unquestioning exactly the right things and persons. You have helped me to understand the importance of discipline, compliance, integrity and commitment- the core human values. You play the role of a 'Mukhiya', the guardian.*

22. **Mr. Sanjay Pandey** |Vice-President, Renowned Indo-Spanish MNC|2020-Till Date| *For being such a good human with an honest and sincere concern for people in need. Your tenure of close to*

three decades and experience with the organization matches what my age is and says a lot about the effort you have put in developing the process and people together

23. **Ms. Neerja Goswami** |Vice-President, Renowned Indo-Spanish MNC|2020-Till Date| *For appreciation, words of praise and patience in tough times. You are a lead by example of commitment by never letting the business obligation fade away even when you lost someone very close to you.*

24. **Mr. J.K. Akash** |Vice-President, Renowned Indo-Spanish MNC|2020-Till Date| *For being grounded, imbibing motivation and positivity. The kind of approach you have towards team is remarkable and one to be graduated from. You serve as a role model for many and have developed incredible leaders under your guidance. I look up to you as a person with whom I can discuss my problems with the assurance to be gifted with solution.*

25. **Mr. C.N. Chander** |Vice-President, Renowned Indo-Spanish MNC|2020-Till Date| *For being humane with everyone. The kind of treatment you give to your fellow colleagues and sub-ordinates deserves to be replicated by every leader. You value, respect and understand the time constraints faced by others, which is a rare quality to find.*

26. **Mr. Palak Jain** |Finance Controller, Renowned Indo-Spanish MNC|2020-Till Date| *For trusting me and being witty with your work. The kind of*

feedback employees give about you is an amazing feat to achieve. You prove that age is just a number with great achievements & experience at such a young age. You handle the backbone for business and that is as giving 'oxygen to businesses'.

27. **Mr. Ashish Singh** |Sr. Manager, Renowned Indo-Spanish MNC|2020-Till Date| *For being so optimistic and your communication skills are of such genre that people look up to match. A special mention for you for the feedback that you provided on writing the introduction of this Ride is so far the best one. It helped me to re-think and create more precision. The effort that you put in reading the introduction and writing the feedback in detail is priceless for me.*

28. **Ms. Charika Gandhi** |**Head Of Business Development and Strategic Alliances at a renowned company @ Dubai**|2021 - Till date| *For being a leader. You helped me by first of all accepting a request from an unknown and respected my thoughts. You have given me great insights about marketing, cover page design and also the timing to launch this journey. The best gift that a person can give is `time` and you have given me the greatest gift and not one but as many times I asked for including the video that I insisted to shoot about the upcoming female generation. At such a young age you have achieved great heights and have inspired me to work even harder. And If I have to say something personal, I would say - besides being a true professional and ambitious human, you are so beautiful the way you look, think and*

behave with an ingredient of acceptance and being grounded. Besides everything, you have the Indian values despite living in an alien country that is absolutely amazingly attractive.

You may find the link to the video on YouTube.

29. **Nishtha Shrivastava** |Miss Asia International 2021, Miss India Shining Star 2020, Indian Finalist for Miss Asia International 2021, Author of Amazon – Best Selling Novel "Rakshabandhan – The fading binds of faith" | 2021 - Till date| *For being a FeDer (Female Leader), you have worked hard and inspired me a lot and specially with the humility and the energy that you possess. Wish you all the best for your future endeavors and accepting my request to shoot a video. By the time you read this, I believe we would have shot the video we planned and may be completed the execution of some projects together.*

You may find the link to the video on YouTube.

30. **Ms. Swati:** |Sr. Designer| August 2021 – Till date |*For preparing the amazing cover design for this book. People appreciated me for the cover design, but it was actually you who should get all the praise and appreciation. So I pass all those beautiful lines to you.*

31. **Mr. Syyed** |2021| *For accepting the manuscript and Getting the 'Expedition' published. Moreover, thank you for bearing with me for a year and following up with me. This shows your interest, dedication and passion towards writing.*

नमस्तेसदावत्सलेमातृभूमेत्वयाहिन्दुभूमेसुखंवर्धितोहम्।
महामङ्गलेपुण्यभूमेत्वदर्थेपतत्वेषकायोनमस्तेनमस्ते।।

हिंदी अनुवाद

हे वात्सल्यमयी मातृभूमि, तुम्हें सदा प्रणाम करता हूँ। इस मातृभूमि ने अपने बच्चों की तरह प्रेम और स्नेह दिया है।हमें इस सुख पूर्वक हिन्दू भूमि पर में बड़ा हुआ हूँ।यह भूमि मंगलमय और पुण्य भूमि है।इस भूमि के लिए में अपने नश्वर शरीर को मातृभूमि के लिए अर्पण करते हुए इस भूमि को बारबार प्रणाम करता हूँ।

Easy to read Translation

He vaatsaly mayee maatr bhoomi, tumhen sada pranaam karata hoon. Is maatrbhoomi ne apane bachchon kee tarah prem aur sneh diya hai. hamen is sukhapoorvak hindoo bhoomi par mein bada hua hoon. Yah bhoomi mangalamay aur punyabhoomi hai. Is bhoomi ke lie mein apane nashvar shareer ko maatrbhoomi ke lie arpan karate hue is bhoomi ko baar baar pranaam karata hoon.

ENGLISH TRANSLATION

I bow to you always, O mother land of love. This motherland has given love and affection like its children. We have grown up on this happily Hindu land. This land is auspicious and holy land. For the sake of this land, I bow to this land again and again, while offering my mortal body to the motherland.

Chapter 1
India @ 75 r.p.m

https://www.business-standard.com/article/companies/i-predict-that-the-21st-century-is-going-to-be-indian-century-jeff-bezos-121020302037_1.html

"I predict that the 21st century is going to be the Indian century. The dynamism, the energy… everywhere I go here, I meet people who are working in self-improvement and growth. This country has something special, democracy," Bezos had said during his India visit last year."

- **Jeff Bezos, Amazon founder and Chief Executive**

Let us give ourselves a promising head start now and before that, let us prepare first.

While trying to figure out the inception of the piece of my mind that you are holding in your hand right now, I was wondering about how to craft an appealing start to the book that will keep us (both you and me) interested and engaged to pen it down and read. Interestingly, I had never planned that I would be writing this 'here'. And by 'here', I mean a beautiful hotel room in New Delhi (the best part I didn't have to pay a single penny. Hhahahhaha!) Wondering why and how? *(It is a secret, connect with me personally to know or else if I tell you, my secret will be revealed...shhhhhh*) The room was filled with pin drop silence that helped me to connect to myself. The only thing accompanying me was the shrilling rhythm coming out from the AC vents with a sharp cool breeze blowing, which gave me the feeling of sitting beside a river.

To make it more vivid, while writing this, I am right now sitting with a towel wrapped (gives me a relaxed feeling, as I am 'ventilated' from top to bottom that allows the circulation of air throughout every part of my body hahahhaha...... *hey!! I can see that cute smile on your face right now, keep smiling and read*), white paper, cup of coffee, water bottle, a blue pen, my mobile phone (of Course on Flight Mode!) curtains wide open to allow the day light to enlighten my mind and the keyboard that goes 'tak tak tak' at a supersonic speed and when people around see me going 'tak tak tak',they scream"*watch out boy, don't misbehave with the laptop, it may catch fire with the speed with which you are typing and please don't show your martial arts skills on the laptop, it is to be handled delicately*". Long story short,

and yes before I forget to mention, another accompaniment was there as a part of river, the rhythmic sound of drops of water from the washroom tap that said-'*tap tap tap*'or as I heard"*Go Rahul, Go Rahul, Go Rahul, You can do it. Go Rahul, Go Rahul, Go Rahul. You can do it!*" and so on. I would urge you to feel the cool breeze, the drops of water or perhaps the current of water as if you are sitting beside a river and mountain, as your two accompaniments while you embark on this journey. Usually, I love to sit in the Nature`s lap to do my creative cravings. Places close to nature like a lake, mountain, river, tall trees (through which I will take you through on this Journey gradually when I unfold things for you) allows me to meet the *'my someone special - The Real Me'*. Using the infinite power of imagination let us believe we are sitting in Nature`s lap and let us get set and go!! Let us rock together.

After using all my mental faculties and muscles, I thought what could be a better way to start by talking about none other than our mother land, our own country and its riches in a fresh cuisine of writing. I am sure you will agree with me. I am right, or am I right?

FEDERs of the 21st Century

FEDERS- (Female-Leaders), (Feder actually means feather). This is so true to be accurate. They already have their feathers widespread and I am sure you will recognize the upcoming lines or at least must have heard a gossip around.

https://www.hindustantimes.com/india-news/sneha-dubey-meet-the-ifs-officer-who-gave-fiery-response-to-imran-khan-at-un-101632551532881.html

https://economictimes.indiatimes.com/news/india/india-slams-pak-pm-imran-khan-at-unga-says-pakistan-is-arsonist-disguising-itself-as-fire-fighter/videoshow/86500392.cms

https://www.ndtv.com/india-news/unga-india-in-right-of-reply-to-imran-khans-address-to-un-general-assembly-says-pakistan-globally-recognised-for-openly-supporting-and-arming-terroris-2552977

"We exercise our Right of Reply to one more attempt by the leader of Pakistan to tarnish the image of this August Forum by bringing in matters internal to my country, and going so far as to spew falsehoods on the world stage," – These were the words of a young educated and fiery FEDER nurtured by India, Sneha Dubey, First Secretary and an IFS officer at UN General Assembly on Friday, 24th September 2021

Giving a blistering response to Imran Khan at UN, she added *"Pakistan holds the ignoble record of hosting the largest number of terrorists proscribed by the UNSC (United Nations Security Council). Osama Bin Laden got shelter in Pakistan. Even today, Pakistan leadership glorifies him as a "martyr".*

Continuing her speech in the most assertive way, she exclaimed, *Pakistan is an "arsonist" disguising itself as a "fire-fighter", and the entire world has suffered because of its policies as the country nurtures terrorists in its backyard. "Regrettably, this is not the first time the leader of Pakistan has misused platforms provided by the UN to propagate false and malicious propaganda against my country, and seeking in vain to divert the world's attention from the sad state of his country where terrorists enjoy free pass while the lives of ordinary people, especially those belonging to the minority communities, are turned upside down."*

"Member States are aware that Pakistan has an established history and policy of harbouring, aiding and actively supporting terrorists. This is a country that has been globally recognized as one openly supporting, training, financing and arming terrorists as a matter of State policy. It holds the ignoble record of

hosting the largest number of terrorists proscribed by the UN Security Council," added Ms Dubey.

"Unlike Pakistan, India is a country with free media and an independent judiciary that keeps a watch and protects our Constitution, Pluralism is a concept which is very difficult to understand for Pakistan which constitutionally prohibits its minorities from aspiring for high offices of the State. The least they could do is introspect before exposing themselves to ridicule on the world stage,"

She also strongly reiterated that the entire Union Territories of Jammu & Kashmir and Ladakh *"were, are and will always be an integral and inalienable part of India". "This includes the areas that are under the illegal occupation of Pakistan. We call upon Pakistan to immediately vacate all areas under its illegal occupation".*

Khan in his address spoke about the 2019 decision of India to abrogate Article 370 as well as the death of pro-Pakistan separatist leader Syed Ali Shah Geelani. "The worst and most pervasive form of Islamophobia now rules India," Khan said in an address, delivered by video due to Covid precautions.

With this incident, the world can now imagine the kind of education, culture, and conducive environment India provides and possess for our females. Ours is a country which we call our "Motherland". It is for some good reason.

Learnings from The Paralympics

Today 5th September, 2021, the teacher's day, blessed by the almighty to get this peaceful time to watch news of the heroics of the youth towards medals tally at Tokyo Paralympics makes me even prouder than ever before to be an Indian. *Wish I could too, win a treasury of medals for my country or may be still I can and I will, who knows.* For you, I am going to bring the unforgettable learning from the lives of able-bodied athletes.

https://www.indiatoday.in/sports/other-sports/story/tokyo-paralympics-india-medal-tally-19-gold-5-sport-wise-list-of-athletes-1849369-2021-09-05

CITIUS ALTIUS FORTIUS – (Faster Higher Stronger), this is the Olympic motto that expresses the aspirations of the Olympic movement. In the following coming lines, we will restrict ourselves to Paralympics, though both the formats remain close to my heart and there is one of my secrets related to Olympics. Ssshh....not to be revealed now. May be in the next book venture. But yes I can at least tell that it is something big.

Let me straight away take you all to an inspirational journey with the destination as unforgettable learnings from the event of Paralympics.India scripted its best-ever medals tally in the Japanese capital, bringing home 19 medals, 15 more than their previous count. As many as 5 gold medals were won and 8 silver medals came the country's way.

India had won only 12 medals from 1968 to 2016 and now what a feat to return home with a treasury of 19 medals from a single event. As a package, we won 8 medals in athletics, 5 medals in shooting, and 4 medals in badminton at the Tokyo Paralympics. Summing up, we won 5 gold medals, 8 silver medals and 6 bronze medals, finishing within the top 25 at the Para Games in the Japanese capital.

India's tally of 19 is also the Country's best at a multi-sport world event, going past the tally of 13 registered at the Summer Youth Olympics in 2018. The record tally in Paralympics comes after the able-bodied athletes scripted history at the Tokyo Olympics, winning 7 medals, their best-ever tally at the Olympics.

My area of interest here is to understand – what goes inside their mind when they practice over the years, perform under such a pressure, struggle and finally succeed, I wish to crack that code so that it can be replicated and transmitted to the upcoming performers for future and this way I am sure we will surpass our own best performance and move upwards and onwards. There must exist a "theory of everything" and there must be a common thread that binds them all or "something" that exists in all the winners. I intuitively think that this code cracking thing will be the topic for my next book venture, but for now I have only covered in the following lines, *Sports Psychology: Inside the champions Mind*. Anyways, moving on,

India finished within the top 25 in the medal table at the Tokyo Paralympics, going past their previous best

by 15 medals. In fact, India had only 19 athletes at the Rio Paralympics where they won 4 medals.
A lot was expected of India's largest contingent at the Paralympics -- a 54 strong unit -- and the para-athletes lived up to the hype, winning medals at will in Tokyo. It all started with a table tennis medal with Bhavinaben Patel becoming the first Indian to win a table tennis medal at the Paralympics. It ended with two badminton players winning medals as Krishna Nagar won a historic gold in the men's singles SH6 category and Suhas Yathiraj, an IAS officer, winning silver in the SL4 category.

There were multiple medalists as well for India as Avani Lekhara won a gold medal and a bronze medal in shooting while Singhraj took a silver and bronze in shooting. Notably, Avani was the India's flag-bearer at the Tokyo Paralympics closing ceremony on Sunday after becoming the first Indian woman gold medalist at the Paralympics history.

Full list of India's medalists from Tokyo Paralympics

1. Avani Lekhara - Gold - Women's 10m Air Rifle Standing SH1
2. Pramod Bhagat - Gold - Men's singles SL3 badminton
3. Krishna Nagar - Gold - Men's singles SH6 badminton
4. Sumit Antil - Gold - Men's Javelin Throw F64
5. Manish Narwal - Gold - Mixed 50m Pistol SH1
6. Bhavinaben Patel - Silver - Women's Singles Class 4 Table Tennis
7. Singhraj - Silver - Mixed 50m Pistol SH1
8. Yogesh Kathuniya - Silver - Men's Discus F56
9. Nishad Kumar - Silver - Men's High Jump T47

10. Mariyappan Thangavelu - Silver - Men's High Jump T63
11. Praveen Kumar - Silver - Men's High Jump T64
12. Devendra Jhajharia - Silver - Men's Javelin F46
13. Suhas Yathiraj - Silver - Men's Singles Badminton SL4
14. Avani Lekhara - Bronze - Women's 50m Rifle 3 Positions SH1
15. Harvinder Singh - Bronze - Men's Individual Recurve Archery
16. Sharad Kumar- Bronze - Men's High Jump T63
17. Sundar Singh Gurjar -Bronze- Men's Javelin Throw F46
18. Manoj Sarkar - Bronze - Men's Singles Badminton SL3
19. Singhraj - Bronze - Men's 10m Air Pistol SH1

Sport-wise tally of India's medals at Tokyo Paralympics

1. Athletics - 8
2. Shooting - 5
3. Badminton - 4
4. Archery – 1

Let me ask you all, which sport would you let your child pursue or as a matter of fact, you yourself will pursue? If I had to answer that, I think I would love to go for shooting.

I leave the onus of answering the above question to you and your children. I am concerned here, as when it comes to performing yourself or letting your child take part in sports or Olympics, would you allow your child to go for it? Think on the lines of why and why Not?

Here I would like to highlight that, we love to clap for the performers and the winners. Don't you think your happiness would be exponentially multiplied and compounded if you get a chance to clap for your own child? Why don't we allow our own children to perform?

So the answer that you just whispered, I could clearly hear is "STRUGGLE AND THE PAIN". I am right or am I? We love to see the gain but what about the pain and the price that needs to be paid? The pain is worth taking I believe and urge you all to participate yourself and allow your children to pursue sports at any level and you may be surprised what it can do to you and your children.

Even if you don't think for such a big stage like Olympics, a marriage with sports in life can do wonders in our performance both personally and professionally as it has astounding effects on the functioning of the brain and the body. This is very well highlighted by Mr. J.K. Akash, VP of a renowned Indo-Spanish Organization. I did an interview with him and he specially highlighted this point. So I would urge you all to take a break from reading, sip a cup of coffee and watch the video @

https://www.youtube.com/watch?v=Vbu2O1C_IsA

As the Journey is towards learning, let me highlight top learnings from para-athletes. They are blessed with special abilities and are a step ahead from their counterparts who are not specially-abled. It is time we shower love and affection to their perseverance and winning attitude. Let us first understand how the idea of Olympics for the specially-abled came into being.

In 1948, there was a meeting among World War II British soldiers. The top leaders brought an idea as to why not bring games for the soldiers who had been injured and became specially abled. This was the inception of the mega event. In the year 1960 was held the first Rome Paralympics. In 1972, Indian team participated. In the beginning only soldiers and few general citizens were allowed to take part in the event but towards the 21st century it became one of the sports mega events.

So here we go, 5L*5P, i.e. *Five learnings from 5 Paralympians.*
This learning comes from a renowned RJ, RJ Kartik who has consistently inspired me with his videos on social media platforms, I regularly watch him in my *Golden Hours (About which you will learn later on in some chapter.)*

1. **Bounce Back** :

   Learning from the life of Avni Lekhra:
   At just a tender age of 19, this year she will be completing 20. She has a heart of lion blessed by courageous parents. She had a life turning event. In 2012, his father, Mr. Praveen Lekhra, who worked in Dhaulpur (Rajasthan), was going from Jaipur to Dhaulpur. Unfortunately, the family met a car accident. Everyone was injured and Avni had to be hospitalized for 3 months as she suffered injuries in back bone. She had no option other than to spend her

time on wheelchair, as she couldn't walk anymore.

His father didn't let her move into depression and negativity. He made it sure that she gets enough motivation. He gifted her, the autobiography of Abhinav Bindra, "A shot at history, My obsessive journey to Olympic gold" to read. Before I progress on this further, I must tell you that I ordered this book right away, and to tell you more I have already started practicing for 10m Air rifle. The book is amazing I must say. It was magically inspiring. Her father always tried to imbibe her interest towards sports.

Initially, Avni started with archery but was not able to pull back and shoot due to weakness. As she was reading Abinav Bindra`s book, she developed an interest in Shooting. Gradually she started training with her father`s help and even Covid`19 couldn't stop her to practice. While the shooting range was closed during the pandemic, Avni didn't stop and was stubborn enough to keep up her practice. Her father had to arrange something digital at home to practice.

And the result of this stubborn and persevering nature was the result at the Tokyo Paralympics, the podium and the stadium resounded with our National Anthem. It was her sheer not giving up attitude that helped us to win Gold in 10 m air rifle. She is the first Indian woman athlete to win Gold in the Paralympics. Not only that now she has also become the brand

Ambassador for the campaign "Beti Padhao Beti Bachao" in Rajasthan.

She is the first FEDER (**FE**male lea**DER**) I mentioned whom you met in this journey and what a moment of inspiration. While writing this I couldn't help myself crying with happiness. I wish may be someday I will be able to meet her.

2. **Never say, why did God choose me for problems? Say, God chooses only those who are capable of coming out of it and conquering fears.**

Learning from the life of Sumit Antil
His journey has been among the toughest. His father, late Shri Ramkumar Sahab who was in Air Force, passed away in 2007. Sumit is the youngest among his siblings of four including him. The turning point: on 5th January, 2015, when he was in 12th Standard, he was en route to his commerce coaching class, he met an accident with a truck loaded with cement packs. The truck hit his bike with brutal force and he was dragged along with his bike to a good distance. He lost one of his legs in this accident after being hospitalized for months.

In 2016, his mother took him to Pune for prosthetic leg surgery. Sumit never said that he had lost something as explained by his mother Mrs. Nirmala Devi, co-incidentally my grandmother`s name. Gradually he pursued his interest towards sports, winning several medals. The biggest motivation came when

Neeraj Chopra won Gold for India in Javelin throw. Sumit says that Neeraj has motivated him tons.

And if we talk about his performance at Tokyo Olympics 2021, he made world record by bettering his own performance or should I say ***his only completion was he himself.***

3. **Convert taunt into thriving. Use those taunts to fuel your dreams.**

   Learning from the life of Devendra Jhajaria
   His story starts when he was 8 years old, he was trying to climb a tree and a high tension wire caught his hand which resulted in later amputating his left hand from the elbow. He was not allowed to move outside his house to be safe from the taunting of the society. He wanted to play and also while spending time at ground, he asked kids to allow him to experience javelin throw.
   He was laughed at by the kids. That didn't stop him and he started practice at his home. He studied at a Government School at Ratanpura School.

   He won gold in Athens in 2004, then again gold in 2016 and then further silver medal in 2021 Tokyo Paralympics. Her wife, also a kabbadi player says, the achievements that Devendra has done outshines what could be achieved with both the hands and is equivalent to thousand hands put together.

4. **Family Support is the fuel for biggest achievements.**

Learning from the life of Nishad Kumar.
He hails from Oni, Himachal. He won a silver medal for India with 2.6 m high Jump. He dedicates his medal to his parents and is a story of sacrifice of his parents including him. In Nishad`s own words, they didn't have a farm land or cultivable area so they worked at someone else`s land.

Their parents couldn't afford three meals a day but made sure that their son, Nishad and daughter get full meals. Their parents told them to focus on studies and not to be bothered by struggles and that they have to change the future. The turning point came in his life when Nishad was 8 years old; he lost his left land while working with a grass cutting machine. Again, with taunts he fuelled his dreams without having proper resources of good pair of shoes, kit etc.

The hunger for conquering the dreams was far more severe than the hunger for food. And the thing to note here for all of us is that behind every big feat there is a **support system** from parents, seniors, friends forevery one of us. Greater the support system, greater is the size and intensity of success. Are we proving enough support to our budding and future champions? I leave this question for you to answer. Before asking our youth to perform well, I think it is time to ask ourselves whether we as a support system are ready to support them emotionally, financially and socially.

5. Never lose the sight of your dreams, no matter what.

Learning from the life of Sundar Singh Gurjar.
He wanted to be an athlete since beginning. He hails from agrarian land, Karauli, Rajasthan. He was so notorious in his childhood that he aimed at pitcher (Matka) carried by village women. Interestingly his parents said if you want to do this, do it nicely to his amazement. His teacher started giving him training in javelin throw in school and developed his infinite fascination and interest with sports.

He was already an athlete and was preparing for Olympics. In 2016, he was at a friend's house, a turnaround came when during a storm in the evening, his left hand accidently was amputated by a tin shed that could not bear the strong winds and met his the champions hand.

He never lost the sight of his dreams and now Olympics dreams shifted to Paralympics but the dream of becoming a successful athlete was intact. He reached in the top list in 2016 Paralympics with top performance. So far so good but unfortunately, when his name was announced on call, he was late by 52 seconds and was disqualified. 5 years pain couldn't be converted into gain due to 52 seconds.

Finally he won bronze for India, in 2021 Tokyo Olympics. That may be a bronze but the will power shines more than a gold medal.

So we usually exclaim "we don't have time""I am going through a tough time". "Monetary loss or loss of loved ones." What is your excuse not to do the things that you have always wished to do?

I leave this up to you to self-introspect, get up and get set go! Get up from the dirt,flirt with opportunities, shirt up the sleeves, check up from the neck up and just do it!

- *Sports Psychology: Getting inside the Mind of a Champion*

Before you start, you must also get to know precisely what goes inside the mind of champions in preparation, perseverance and winning. Its understanding will not only benefit you in sports but also in personal and professional excellence. Most importantly how do I know it? I am a certified CBT (Cognitive Behavioral Therapist) Practitioner and an avid psychology enthusiast. Perhaps, understanding of human brain and why an individual behaves in a certain way is the best subject that I have ever been interested in. My understanding was even more magnified during my *golden hours* (you will get to know about golden hours later in the journey), by exactly the right person to explain and help me understand in detail the mental preparation, process and what it takes to be a champion along with dealing with failures and setbacks.

I was amazed to watch him explain with ease and with such a precision in one of the ted talks that I adore and wish to be at the platform one day. I must highlight the platform as it has been one of my key accompaniments in this beautiful journey since 2012. About TEDx, x = independently organized event in the spirit of ideas worth spreading, TEDx is a program of local, self-organized events that bring people together to share a TED-like experience. At a TEDx event, TEDTalks video and live speakers combine to spark deep discussion and connection in a small group. These local, self-organized events are branded TEDx, where x = independently organized TED event. The TED Conference provides general guidance for the TEDx program, but individual TEDx events are self-organised.* (*Subject to certain rules and regulations)

The amazing person is Martin Hagger, Professor of Psychology at Curtin University. His areas of expertise are social, health, sport and exercise psychology. He is involved in numerous research projects nationally and internationally with a focus on motivation and behavior change. And as I am a CBT Practitioner, his explanation had mandatorily been one of my areas of interest. Who could have been better to explain about Sports Psychology?

Martin provides an overview of the kinds of techniques that elite athletes use to prepare psychologically for their sport, give details of the scientific research into these techniques and how they work, and how the techniques might be used by competitive athletes and coaches to maximize performance. Not only sports, I feel a clear understanding and awareness is definitely going to help us all in personal and professional excellence also.

According to him, sports psychology is the study and practice of mental preparation, awareness and practice of techniques and strategies to maximize performance with a cushion of techniques that helps to deal with stress and coping with setbacks.

He explains the factors linked to success in sports:

1. Motivation
2. Confidence
3. Performance Knowledge – `total` sport
4. Routines
5. Anxiety Management.

Apart from performance at sports, don't you think such factors can certainly help in professional excellence?

Further he explains, champions are good at getting in the right frame of mind.

Ok, so now we know `what` the factors are. I have a good news for you. You are also going to get to know `how` do they do it and also not a very good news for you. I will not be able to give you the `why`. You have to curate your own `why`. I can of course help you out to reach your `why` behind your goal. On your marks? Get set go!

1. **Motivation**

   We must understand that Goals that define an athlete.

   How to define a goal? You may have seen this before and moreover there is an extension to it.

   S: Specific
   M: Meaningful
   A: Agreed
   R: Relevant
   T: Time-Specific
   E: Engaging
   R: Recorded

The most important thing to note here is that it is not only the goals you set that matter. It is actually the sub-goals that add up to your ultimate goal. This being said, we must focus on the process (sub-goals) and not only on the end result, though it is equally important to have a vivid end goal. We must not be tempted or overwhelmed by the end goal which conspires against us to let lose focus from our sub-goals.

2. **Confidence**

Secret behind being confident lies in the awareness and understanding of the difference that exists between under confidence, confidence and over confidence.
How to do this is a matter of concern for us here:

- Experience
- Modelling
  - Observation
  - Imagery
  - Self-talk
    - Motivational (`come on`, `you can do this`)
    - Focusing – important cues
    - Calming (e.g: `calm`, `breathe`, `relax`)
- Feedback

3. Anxiety Management

This is where most of us lag and think that stress & anxiety as a natural phenomenon. Yes, no doubt about that, but it is not naturally controlled. We must take ownership to control our anxiety or else it has the potential to ruin all our efforts and play havoc with our body and mind. If you take my words, this is the `first thing first` even before setting up a goal as the goal in itself is going to give you stress sometimes after.

- Relaxation Techniques:
    - Breathing
    - Stretching
    - Muscles
    - Music
    - Meditation

Wondering that I didn't cover point number 3 & 4 written in the `how` section i.e performance knowledge and routines?

We must understand that there is no `one size fits all` routine for us. We must be specific while defining our routine and acquiring performance knowledge. If you want to really understand and set specific routines you may get in touch with me for hitting the bull's eye. To help you with the visual explanation of the sports psychology, you may visit the link below:

https://www.youtube.com/watch?v=yG7v4y_xwzQ

If you can recollect the title of the chapter, it was, India @ 75 r.p.m, where r.p.m usually means revolutions per minute in automobile industry. But here I like to put it as `revolutions` per minute that happens in our country. I read this title in one of the renowned newspapers.

India has come far and we have celebrated 75 years of independence. We must self-reflect to see where do we stand after 75 years of independence and where are we heading. This should give the proudest of feeling to live in such a country that welcomes everyone with open arms.

- ***The Sanskrit Effect***

https://www.thehindu.com/sci-tech/science/the-sanskrit-effect-and-how-rigorous-memorising-helps-the-memory/article22436878.ece

The 'Sanskrit effect' and how rigorous memorising helps the memory - JANUARY 13, 2018

I read these lines in one of the leading newspaper – The Hindu, and was amazed to read this. Let me share some interesting facts.

The article read as- Considerable excitement has been triggered through email and social media across India due to a recent "observation" reported by one Dr James Hartzell in the journal *Scientific American*.

This neuroscientist has coined the term "The Sanskrit effect." He writes that memorising Vedic mantras increases the size of brain regions associated with cognitive function such as memory (both short-term and long-term). He writes in his report that Indian tradition holds that rigorously memorising and reciting mantras enhances memory and thinking. In order to test this idea, Hartzell (and his colleagues from the University of Trento in Italy) teamed up with Dr Tanmay Nath and Dr Nandini Chatterjee Singh of the National Brain Research Centre (NBRC) at Manesar in Haryana.

They chose to study 42 volunteers — 21 professionally qualified Sanskrit Pandits (aged around 22) who have been trained full-time daily for 7 years (total of over 10,000 hrs) in their childhood reciting the Shukla Yajurveda. These Pandits were recruited from Vedic

Pandit schools in Delhi. As control, they chose 21 age-matched males, students from a nearby college.

The brains of all the 42 participants were examined using the method called structural magnetic resonance, with the magnetic resonance imaging instrument at NBRC. This method allows the study of the size and shape of individual parts of brain. The so called **grey matter (GM)** of the brain is a region full of neuronal cells, and contains areas involved in muscle control, sensory perception, memory, emotions, speech and decision-making. And connected to it is **white matter (WM)** — bundles of nerve cells that carry signals to GM.

The **hippocampus** is a small organ located within the central region of the brain, and it registers and regulates emotions associated with memory (particularly long-term memory) and has front and back sections. The back part appears associated with better memory and supports recollection of memory. And the **cortex**, which is the outermost layer surrounding the brain (essentially a cover or envelope), with its tightly packed nerve cells, is responsible for higher thought processes such as decision-making.

The Indo-Italian team analysed the brain regions of the 21 Pandits and 21 control volunteers and found some remarkable differences between the two. They found the grey matter in Pandits to be denser and the cortex thicker than in 'controls', and the hippocampus regions, associated with long- and short-term memory was more pronounced. (Interested readers can access this paper free at <http:/dx.doi.org/10.1016/j.neuroimage.2015.07.0

29>). Indeed, a similar experiment, again using Vedic Pandits (this time in Houston, TX, USA), was done earlier by Dr Giridhar Kalamangalam and T. M. Ellmore (accessible free in *Frontiers in Human Neuroscience,* 2014 Oct 20;8:833. doi: 10.3389/fnhum.2014.00833. eCollection 2014), and they too noted thicker cortex in the Pandits than in controls.

Importantly, these changes in the brain are not temporary but stay for long. That means that the power of memory, decision-making, sensory perception and such would last longer in those who were trained earlier. Dr Danker and Dr Anderson, who were studying this aspect, actually titled their 2010 review as "The ghosts of brain states past; remembering reactivates the brain regions engaged during coding" (*Psychol. Bull.,* 136, 87-102. doi: 10.1037/a0017937). Here coding refers to the earlier rigorous practice and memorising.

It is also important to realise that one need not attach any special power to Shukla Yajurveda as a brain enhancer. Fifty years ago, a French scientist noted that Christian monks who chanted the Gregorian Chants have exceptional memory (though no brain scanning methods were available at that time). Further, it need not be verbal or religious chanting at all. It could be visual and spatial training too. Dr Eleanor Maguire and colleagues studied the brain structures of the taxi drivers of London, each one having gone through a vigorous and extensive course called "The Knowledge."

In this course, each driver is taught and had to memorise the spatial location of every street, monument and tourist spot across greater London before being given a taxi driver license. He needs no GPS; it is all in his hippocampus, GM and cortex. (Interested readers may access *Proc Natl Acad Sci U S A.* 2000 Apr 11; 97(8): 4398–4403. doi: 10.1073/pnas.070039597). One is also reminded of how the multiplication tables we had learnt by rote in primary school in India comes in handy decades later when we go shopping in stores.

(Incidentally, several years ago, a scientist claimed that listening to the music of the European composer Mozart helps in memory and smartness and termed this the "Mozart Effect". School children were asked to do some tasks while listening to Mozart, and they did better than when Mozart was not played. This led a rush by parents to music stores to buy and play Mozart to their children. Soon enough, it was found that the effect lasts only when the music was played; the kids felt more relaxed and smoothed; after the music stopped, the effect vanished. The Mozart effect did not last long).

These studies also raise the possibility that we may exert or exercise our brains by doing "memory training," even during later life when we are old, and need not have been Pandits, Gregorian monks or London cabbies. Indeed, the paper by A. Engwig and colleagues talks about how systemic mental exercise may induce short-term structural change in the ageing brain (in the journal *Neuroimage* in 2010; short summary accessible at doi:
10.1016/j.neuroimage.2010.05.041). They show memory trainees to have increased cortical thickness

than controls do. Just as physical exercise helps our brawn, mental exercise helps our brain. So, let us seniors do word puzzles and games, learn (relearn) languages, practice music, chant Gregorian or Vedic texts (but in the proper chanda or metre), and our brains can still be young.
dbala@lvpei.org

- ***Sanskrit Week***

https://currentaffairs.adda247.com/india-celebrates-sanskrit-week-2021-from-august-19-to-25/

I am yet to figure out if this is the effect that has helped me to be more efficient at my venture as I have been a regular Sanskrit reader which you might have discovered with the phrases that I have tried to present to you in this journey.

In 2021, India is observing the Sanskrit Week from August 19 to August 25, 2021, to promote, popularize and cherish the importance of this ancient language. In 2021, Sanskrit Day was celebrated on August 22, 2021. The day is celebrated on the full moon day of the month of Shravan, which also marks the occasion of Raksha Bandhan each year. World Sanskrit Day was first declared in 1969, by the Indian Government on the occasion of Raksha Bandhan.

https://www.hindustantimes.com/india-news/pm-modi-sends-message-on-world-sanskrit-day-all-you-need-to-know-about-the-language-101629606416445.html

By hindustantimes.com | Written by Ayshee Bhaduri | Edited by Meenakshi Ray, Hindustan Times, New DelhiUPDATED ON AUG 22, 2021 10:02 AM IST

Shri Narendra Modi had also sent a message on World Sanskrit Day. World Sanskrit Day is celebrated on Shravana Poornima every year, and this year it was on August 22.Prime Minister Narendra Modi took to Twitter on Sunday to mark the occasion of World Sanskrit Day. Sanskrit is an ancient Indian language and belongs to the Indo-European group of languages. Sanskrit is often referred to as the language of the gods and is made of the words sáṃ, meaning together, good, well, perfected, and kṛ ta, meaning made, formed and work. When used together connotes something that is well-formed or perfected.

World Sanskrit Day is celebrated on Shravana Poornima every year, and this year it was on August 22. It was celebrated for the first time in the year 1969 after the Union ministry of education issued notifications to state and central governments.

https://en.wikipedia.org/wiki/World_Sanskrit_Day

World Sanskrit Day, also known as **Vishva-samskrita-dinam** (Sanskrit: विश्वसंस्कृतदिनम्, romanized: *Vịvasaṃsktadinam*), is an annual event focused around the ancient Indian language of Sanskrit that incorporates lectures about the language and is aimed to promote its revival and maintenance. It is celebrated on Shraavana poornima, that is the full moon day of the Shraavana month in the Hindu calendar. The Sanskrit organisation Samskrita Bharati is involved in promoting the day.

Shravani Purnima i.e. Raksha Bandhan is considered to be the festival of remembrance and worship of sages and worship for their dedication. In Vedic literature it was called Shravani. On this day, before the study of Vedas in Gurukulas, *Yajñopavita* - sacred thread - is worn. This ceremony is called Upanayana or Upakarma Sanskar. The old*Yajñopavita* is also changed on this day. Priests also tie raksha-sutras to the hosts.

Rishis are the original source of Sanskrit literature, hence Shravani Purnima is celebrated as Rishi Parv and World Sanskrit Day. This day was chosen because the academic year in ancient India started on this day. On this day the students start the study of Vedas in the gurukulas. From the full moon of the month of Paush to the full moon of the month of Shraavana, the studies are stopped to learn other vedantic scriptures. This tradition is still unbroken in modern Vedic schools.

In 1969, the Ministry of Education of Government of India issued instructions to celebrate Sanskrit Day at the Central and State levels. Since then Sanskrit day is celebrated all over India. On this occasion, Sanskrit Kavi Sammelan, writer's seminar, students' speeches and verse recitation competition etc. are organized, through which Sanskrit students, poets and writers get a proper platform.

Nowadays Sanskrit Day is celebrated with great enthusiasm, not only in India but also worldwide. The contribution of the Central and State Government of India is also noteworthy in this. The week in which Sanskrit day falls is celebrated as Sanskrit week for some years. Due to the declaration of Sanskrit as the official language in Uttarakhand, there are different programs and competitions in Sanskrit language every day in Sanskrit week. The basic objective of celebrating Sanskrit Day and Sanskrit Week is to spread the word of Sanskrit language.

Happy Vishva-samskrita-dinam to all!!!!

Chapter 2: Historical Present of the Future

- The Quarantine Era

"If you ever dreamed of playing for the millions around the world, now is your chance. Play inside, play for the world"

- ***A tribute to the heroes***

Such striking lines I found over a LinkedIn page as an advertisement by Nike in times of crisis. This was enough that motivated me to stay at home during the outbreak of COVID-19, we just surpassed and are still trying our best to manage with precautionary measures.

Have you ever wondered that ***a crisis is the indication to something great?*** If you don't believe this statement, the COVID`19 crisis is a living proof. Let me take you all on a journey that we have all been a part of from early 2020. We have been surely a participant of *historical present of the future*. The achievements during this period and due to its outbreak will superimpose and outshine the losses. Though the fatalities have been humungous, but we are still breathing and that is the greatest achievement above all the losses.

I would like to first start by a heart-warming praise and a sincere thank you to all those who have gone beyond their normal service to prove that humans have the power of doing anything. The power of humanity, the power of faith, the power of being united in diversity to the power of being united in isolation.

The endless list includes:

1. The first and foremost ***our farmers*** who despite all the difficulties continued to invest their sweat and equity by feeding us in the tough times. We should all thank them, the Reroes (**Re**al life He**roes**)
2. All the ***medical staffs & doctors*** who risked their life, sacrificed on their sleep and worked tirelessly to restore humanity and peace.
3. All the ***ground level support staffs*** who assiduously kept working and risked their breathe to clean up and sanitize so that the world can breathe.
4. All the ***police personnel*** who went beyond their routine duty to restore equilibrium of life.
5. All the ***Ministers & Politicians*** who actively took charge and showed us the way.
6. All the ***Common men and women*** who followed all the rules to ensure our win over the COVID-19 pandemic because each one of us matters.

7. All ***the corporate giants*** who supported their employees to allow them WFH (Work From Home) and other preventive measures.
8. All ***the shop owners*** be it small or large who provided the necessities in time of crisis to ensure that the show must go on.
9. All ***the ambulance drivers,*** who diligently drove to hospitals to save patients.
10. All ***the government and private support staffs*** who tirelessly sanitized our country to save humanity.
11. All ***the media professionals*** who worked day in and day out to bring the best of information, keeping in mind the gravity of the pandemic. We must praise for the authenticity and the credibility.
12. All the ***film stars & actors, and individuals*** who have selflessly supported in times of necessity.
13. All the ***NGO`s & Social organizations*** that provide support to the needy.
14. All the ***big corporations*** who mobilized massive amounts of money.
15. All of ***YOU*** to understand the gravity of the outbreak and co-operating with the government as heroes by patiently being at home during the lockdown.

And as I said, the list is endless. Please forgive me if I forgot to mention few names. I will try to cover all in upcoming paragraphs.

This reminds me of a very motivational phrase by Steve Harvey,

"If you are going through hell, keep going. Why would you stop in hell?"

This perfectly connects to what we all have gone through which has been more than a hell, the novel COVID-19. I assume and I am sure that you all already know about the stats and losses all over the world. I am more interested in bringing the ***Positive outlook of the COVID-19.***

It would not be wise if I don't mention the ***Prime Minister of our country, Shri Narendra Modi.*** I would urge you to keep aside politics and see, read this fact as objectively as possible. I don't have nerves to imagine what he might have gone through and still going. Has anyone ever tried to understand his mental state?

Being the Prime Minister, it would not have been an easy task I imagine. He is such a man of patience with precise efforts, it would not be wrong to Praise his efforts. I would love to call him ***KAVIM,*** a Sanskrit word meaning "**the learned or a great scholar."** And I have been lucky enough to be a part of history in the making. During this crisis, I have observed him closely wherein he tried his best to serve as a Guardian of the country.

Let us pause for a moment and thank him for his efforts where he created an atmosphere of festival in such a terrible environment through a very creative approach on 22nd March. Let us relive the moment of JANATA curfew, which was by the people, for the people and of the people in his words. That also reminds me of the preamble of India which starts by saying, "WE. THE PEOPLE OF INDIA..."

And if that feeling didn't last for long and people started to go in despair soon watching everyday news and never-ending fatalities, he again lifted the spirit by announcing a rare event on 5th April 2020. He advised to light candles, lamps, torches and mobile flashlight and to turn off the lights for 9 minutes at 9: 00PM.

I am sure it had nothing to do with failure of power grid or superstition to the logic of number 9, and what not. And I wonder what does the digit 9 has to do with any religion? My mental muscles gave up here with this thought. Can you answer this? I again leave the question with you.

Anyways, at the moment when I was writing these lines, I had just bought enough lamps and candles keeping in the social distance rule, to participate in perhaps the biggest festival of modern India during an pandemic. It was an astounding experience to see our new India with unity in isolation. What I had known our country for years as *Unity in diversity*. But that day brought new lens to see our mother land and why it is unique and called ***The Golden Bird.***

Let us have a look at the steps taken by him and his counterparts to ensure that we defeat the novel COVID-19 and to minimize the damages.

Amid the NOISE of Delhi riots of the Shaheen Bagh incident and other places of north-Eastern Delhi which for a month was another hell before the outbreak of the virus. On 3rd March 2020, Modi Ji, tweeted about leaving social media platform completely or at least for some time for reasons that would take you to the term ***DIGITAL DEMENTIA***, later discussed in detail.

Source: India Today Web Desk
New Delhi
March 16, 2020UPDATED: March 16, 2020 00:30 IST

To serve as an ***antidote to failure,*** Shri. Narendra Modi, on 15th March 2020, called for video meet of the SAARC countries wherein he led the SAARC (South Asian Association for Regional Cooperation) meet, and encouraged the member nations to start working on regional strategy to tackle coronavirus.

Leaders of the state who took part in the video conference were Maldivian President Ibrahim Mohamed Solih, Sri Lankan President Gotabaya Rajapaksa, Bhutanese Prime Minister Lotay Tshering, Bangladeshi Prime Minister Sheikh Hasina, Nepalese Prime Minister K P Sharma Oli and Afghan President Ashraf Ghani. Meanwhile, special assistant to Prime

Minister Imran Khan, Dr Zafar Mirza represented Pakistan. Let me share the quick takeaways.

1) PM Narendra Modi hovered the inkling of a Covid-19 Emergency Fund for SAARC member nations. He pledged USD 10 million (Rs 73.95 crore) to the fund. He also stated that voluntary contributions will allow this fund to help countries affected in South Asia to tide over economic losses, foreign secretaries of SAARC member nations have been asked to take this initiative forward.

2) PM Modi announced that a rapid response team of doctors and specialists has been kept on standby and will be at the disposal of India's neighbors if and when required.

3) India`s PM also offered online training capsules for the emergency response staff in SAARC member nations.

4) As proposed by a number of SAARC leaders, health secretaries and experts from all SAARC member nations will hold a follow-up video conference to discuss and deliberate a graded response action plan to limit the spread of Covid-19.

5) Bangladeshi Prime Minister Sheikh Hasina also told SAARC leaders that Bangladesh will assist other SAARC nations in terms of logistics if required.

6) Trade officials and experts will be consulted to determine the short-term and long-term losses to SAARC member nations and will also be asked to come up with a plan to insulate intra-regional trade and development.

7) PM Modi informed about how India is using an ***Integrated Disease Surveillance Portal (IDSP)*** to identify and monitor those with exposure to the novel coronavirus. He urged his counterparts to make use of the same software.

8) The leaders have agreed to use the SAARC Disaster Management Centre to identify and popularize best practices enabling South Asia to safeguard itself against the pandemic.

9) PM Modi also offered the expertise of the Indian Council of Medical Research (ICMR) to set up a research platform for diagnostic and therapeutic interventions for diseases.

10) Also, a proposal to set up a website with Covid-19 information material in the languages of all SAARC member nations, offered PM Modi.

Following the meet, on 19th March 2020, the PM, addressed the country for a very creative and much needed preventative measure i.e., **the Janta curfew.** (Of the people, by the people and for the people). It was proposed to be served as a giant leap in war against COVID-19. It was a show of ***`Sanyam` and***

`Sankalp` meaning patience and commitment respectively. Consequently, the date was 22nd March 2020 for the curfew.

The highlight being the 5 PM 5 Minutes of ***unity in isolation,*** with the pure and serene sound of conch shells, bells, plates and spoons striking together creating a memorable moment of joy amid such a crisis environment. Everyone from common man to celebrities, from the haves to the have-nots of the society participated and showed what India is known for. Whether we stand ***united in diversity or united in isolation,*** we, the people of India stand united.

Some ground realities were brought forth by the Times Now Group.

1. **Antibiotics** don't work against viruses
2. **The mask prodigy (Though it is debatable)**: only wear a mask if you are sick or have COVID`19 symptoms.
3. Times now stated that there has been **no evidence that pets could also spread the virus.**
4. If **compared to SARS** (Severe acute respiratory syndrome): SARS was more deadly than COVID-19 but less infectious.
5. **The virus may persist on surfaces for a few hours to several days** which makes it exponentially more infectious than its counterparts.

On 24th March 2020, the PM again took charge and imposed the Janata curfew much stricter than before for complete 21 days. It started on 25th March 2020. Such a bold and courageous step I must say. He strongly advised and requested from his heart for **social distancing.** The complete lockdown of the country is one of its kind in the history. It wouldn't be wrong to say that we could witness *"Historical Present of the Future"*. You can well imagine the economic and other related impacts. My mental faculties would even fail to imagine the losses for such a big step. But PM Narendra Modi had the grit to bear the losses that would be worth to save the lives of millions.

Such a stern step was bound to curb the menace of the pandemic. And if you look at the stats, by WHO, the 1st 1 Lakh cases around the world took 67 days, the next 1 lakh in just 11 days and further 1 lakh in staggering 4 days. You can very well imagine the severity of the situation.

And if that was not enough we had a catalyst awaiting around the corner, Tablighi Jamaat workers, where in with due respect to the Muslim community brothers, they may not have the intention of harming our country by the event, but by concealing the facts and then the hide and seek game played was detrimental. So, if you are not courageous enough to take a stand in favor of our country, then I wonder, of what character and stand you are made of? So, always take a stand for your motherland without the appearance of a drop of fear. Later on news of Tablighi Jamaat workers who won the fight against the virus were seen donating plasma. A brave and humane effort. A big praise for all the donors.

Be a man and woman of character and not the one of mere sand. Whether is it staying at home, or raising voice against the atrocities, be it revealing facts or asking questions for the wrong doings. After all as a son & daughter, would you be able to see your motherland being robbed off her clothes right in front of your eyes? I leave onus of the answer with you.

Technology can sometimes be misused against humanity and made us realize that technological advancement also bring its own repercussions. The best example seen here were aftershocks of few rumors that led to the mass exodus of laborers of UP, Bihar and other neighboring states from Delhi. I could not stop myself crying after seeing the pictures of the Indians, hungry for food. People in thousands and unimaginable numbers started migrating back to their native states on feet. The journey was both detrimental for the country as well as the people themselves. Still my manes go berserk by even remembering such heart-wrenching pictures of the mass at bus stops, roads, stations and everywhere.

Technology is indeed powerful but at both the extremes of the good and the evil.

I personally feel pity for the employers who could not care for their employees during adverse times. Investing in people is the best investment. These money-mongers became everything except being human.

In addition, there was another similar incident in Maharashtra where thousands of workers again became victims of rumors that led them to gather in huge numbers. Again a potential catalyst for the COVID-19 spread.

There had been misuse of few famous apps on one side and on the other side we also had seen how we made the best use of technology by launching the ***Aarogya Setu App*** through which I recently downloaded my final jab certificate. The App, that I believe most of you already have on your handsets is aimed at augmenting the initiatives of the Government of India, particularly the Department of Health, in proactively reaching out to and informing the users of the app regarding risks, best practices and relevant advisories pertaining to the containment of COVID-19.

Then came the role of Hydrocholoroquine, a medication used to treat malaria and also ailments like rheumatoid arthritis, lupus, porphyria cutanea tarda. It was experimentally being used as a treatment to the deadly coronavirus. Besides being in the list of World Health Organization`s essential medicines, it is one of the safest and most effective medicines needed in a health system. It was approved for medical use in the US in 1955.

India decided to first take a look at its requirement for the country before exporting offshore. But before India could do this, Mr. Donald Trump, President of the US already had started to lose calm. He, in his known ways attained an autocratic stance, and said to be ready to face similar behavior if India didn't agree on exportation of the essential medicine. And if you look at the stats, India not only catered to its own country`s demand, but also supplied medicines to 55-countries hit by Corona. This was supplied as grants as well as on commercial basis. Some of them like the US, Mauritius, and Seychelles were among the first one to receive the medicine.

India also planned to send the medicine to its neighboring countries like Nepal, Afghanistan, Bhutan, Bangladesh, Maldives Sri Lanka, & Myanmar.

The list also includes Peru, Netherlands, Egypt, Zambia, Armenia Dominican Republic, Oman, Uganda, Burkina Faso, Niger, France, Mali Congo, Zimbabwe, Kazakhstan, Madagascar, Jordan, Kenya, and Nigeria besides many other.

In a step to further curb COVID-19 and to minimize its impact, India was prompted to go for Lockdown 2.0 from 15th April, 2020 with uncomfortable stats. At least India fared so well from its counterparts unlike the US, Italy, Spain and other places where the infections went in lakhs and werenear out of control situation.

Then as much to a test of patience, India was bold enough to go for lockdown 3.0 from 4th May, 2020. The stats show that if it would not have been in place then the figures would roar in lakhs. It also bought time for our country to prepare for the worst days ahead. With a financial boost of a cumulative package of 20 lakh crores as claimed by the Prime

Minister of India, it was a time to spin the economic wheels. And on 14th May, 2020, while we were about to see an end to lockdown 3.0 in a few days or perhaps it may be the dawn of lockdown 4.0, we were expecting the next installment of announcement expected to boost Indian Economy.

So as expected lockdown 4 was implemented with substantial decision making powers vested to the state governments. With much reluctance, states opened up slightly with media houses and experts still in debates whether it was a pragmatic move or not. The pictures were surprising especially the ones of aircrafts. Didn't it seem like entering to a hospital ward rather than airports and aircrafts? In the history of airline operation, it was after a century that in-flight food was not served since its inception.

Fast forwarding it, today I was wondering, when I am sitting on 19th September, 2021, I have an early morning flight to board to Chennai for some official work, would I get my breakfast or not? Luckily things are normal than before now with infection rates declining g and death rate also slowing down, but still we a have a long way to go.

So now while writing this I am inside the flight 35,000 Ft or roughly 10.5 Km above the sea level and as I had guessed it right, I got my meal pack in the sight, with a smile that was bright and yes I could write these lines with a great insight. While writing this and the scene outside is amazing carnation of Nature. `Cotton balls` or to present it more vividly were the infinite cloud blossoming bright with sunlight. I was so lost that I didn't want to take pictures. Instead, the only thing I wanted was to experience the peace and beauty of nature.

And here came another beautiful creation of God. Can u guess it? Umm. I would like you all to give a thought please. A more than beautiful Airhostess with an amazing voice of a nightingale came and explained the stuffs with an exercise of such a confidence that is not easy to exuberate. And to increase my heart rate there was an announcement that due to bad weather we needed to fasten seatbelts. And to keep myself calm, I kept myself focused on Sonam, the airhostess, her voice and her beauty. This is the only sign of warmth as my heart is pounding right now when I am writing this due to not a very good weather.

Then came a voice that helped me smile, feel proud and move over the panic monster. Sonam announced about Amrit Mahotsav, wherein Indian National army was set up in the year 1942 this month. Whereever I am whether on land, water or 35000ft high in the air, I can`t help myself to feel proud about the riches of my motherland.

https://amritmahotsav.nic.in/about.htm
Before I forget to mention, Azadi Ka Amrit Mahotsav is an initiative of the Government of India to celebrate and commemorate 75 years of progressive India and

the glorious history of its people, culture and achievements.

The **Mahotsav is dedicated to the people of India** who have not only been instrumental in bringing India thus far in its evolutionary journey but also hold within them the power and potential to enable Prime Minister Modi's vision of activating India 2.0, fuelled by the spirit of **Atmanirbhar Bharat.**

Azadi ka Amrit Mahotsav is an embodiment of all that is progressive about India's socio-cultural, political and economic identity. The official journey of "Azadi ka Amrit Mahotsav" commences on 12th March, 2021 which starts a 75 week countdown to our 75th anniversary of Independence and will end post a year on 15th August, 2023.

Let us not lose the locus of our focus and get back to the learnings from the recent pandemic.

- ***Unforgettable Learnings from the Crisis***

*1. **Adaptability***

If we have not yet learned the art of adaptability, there cannot be more aptly suited indication to learn this *art of adaptability*. Perhaps this is not a new skill or phenomenon. This very well resembles with what the Epic Bhagvad Gita has since ages inspired within us. I will take the liberty here to present something in our mother tongue "Parivartan sansar ka niyam hai," that means change is the law of nature.

I am sure nobody would have ever imagined such a massive change in all respect, right from our waking up to professional lives, personal relationships to the way we interact with our Mother Nature.

Let us take some examples from different spheres of life during the Quarantine era.

Firstly, a very simple one put here, how many of you had struggled or are still struggling with your daily routines? Just because we couldn't adapt quickly, many of us lost sight of our daily routines that led our days became nights and the nights became days. Waking up all the night to struggle with food habits, poor physical and mental health during the *Quarantine Era*. Yet I must appreciate those who on the flipside improved up on their daily routines with healthy habits of *early to bed, early to rise*.

On our buying behaviors, we have seen how big corporate giants started to lose on their sales target as people then started to spend on only the essential which makes us to conclude that all the years more or less we had developed a habit of spending on non-essential items.

From one of the Indian Corporate Conglomerate, TCS, it was quick enough to plan out strategies to have work from home culture. It realized that with minimum staffing of say around 25-50% of normal staff strength can work from office with others working from home, it could achieve its yearly financial targets. Speaking from a closer futuristic perspective, imagine how many problems this culture will solve if not only the tech giants, but even small and medium enterprises adapt to this new age culture. Gone are the old rules of the game.

I can see potential solutions in decrease in road traffic which in turn would solve pollution problems. It will further help to reduced consumption of electricity and besides other benefits. This can help in cost cutting and also immediate impact on company`s balance sheet.

On a more human level, it will further add up in improving family relationships, where in children will be able to learn some life skills from their parents attending meetings from home. Children can have numerous internship opportunities right at their homes from the most trusted gurus i.e., their parents. Moreover, parents who were left behind with their relationship with technology, can take help from their children who can help them with their youth, full of ideas and creativity. Children can assist their parents with their fresh knowledge and in turn can learn the paradigms of the professional world.

And if people were worried how corporates would adapt. I have an astounding example of if not the greatest but one of the greatest partnerships. It was around $5.7 Billion partnership between Indian Organization Reliance & the American social media behemoth Facebook. Even in times of disaster, the two master minds, Mr. Mukesh Ambani and his counterpart Mark Zuckerberg entered into a big deal which has the potential to upend the entire payment industry in India. Such big organizations were quick and agile enough to adapt to the changing demands of the hour to charter a historic deal. Brave, courageous and what not.

I have just mentioned a few, but there are numerous potential possibilities with the new work culture. It can only be possible if we develop the *art of adaptability*.

So I urge you all to get a hand at this art. The question may come here how to learn this art? All the time we are taught what to learn and not how to learn. But the good news is, you have a detailed answer and explanation to the question of how to learn adaptability. Refer to the chapter "***Learning how to learn,***" of this book.It will help you all to do it very smoothly. And being specific, there is a topic with the name *The 7 States of Mind*. After all, the essence of the book is - *Learning how to learn*.

2. Investing

The best investment you can make, is an investment in yourself.

-Warren Buffet

I am sure you may have heard this phrase somewhere or the other. And the man who said this needs no introduction. I strongly believe that the real meaning of investment is misinterpreted most of the times with the numbers. And why not. It is a human nature. Are you not fascinated by the magical process of learning? I have been a religious preacher of the process of learning once I realized its importance in early childhood. Quickly sharing one of my stories about which you will read later in the book.

All the years of my studies, I was in my own whim of playing and leading a casual life by the tender age of 12, till the time I was not thrown out of one of the top rated schools. After struggling to get enrolled in another school, I had my first encounter with the magical process of learning. It took me complete 1 year to realize the importance. I found the very first love of my life, the process of learning. I was so fascinated with the process that at that tender age I could decide what I will be doing the rest of my life. And to my amazement, my passion for learning has become my profession. This is what prompted me to write this book.

Getting back to the *art of investing,* have you ever thought on investing? This question may create a picture of stock market in your mind. But along with that I am also concerned with the investment in learning & development, personal finance, relationships, etc.

It is this art of all the riches of success and skill that helps us to cope up with adversity that life keeps on presenting us from time to time. The ROI (Return on Investment) proves to always have a positive graph. The investment in learning never lets you down.

Few suggestions on investing areas that will always have positive returns.

i. Learning & Development *(It is magical)*

ii. Relationships
(It is satisfying and emotionally Enriching)

iii. Physical Health
(Doesn't need an explanation, we have seen a fresh spell)

iv. Mental Health
(Learn to take care of your brain and it will take care of the rest)

v. Technology
(Those who had engaged in video call for the first time must have realized)

vi. Finance
(I am not the right person to explain this, but I will surely suggest
few superb books here that will help you.)

For Personal finance you can refer to books, like

- Think and Grow Rich by, Napoleon Hill.
- Rich Dad Poor Dad, by Robert Kiyosaki & Sharon Lechter.
- The Richest Man in Babylon, by George Samuel Classon

And for those who are interested in stock market can refer to some classics like

- The Security Analysis by, Benjamin Graham & David Dodd
- The Intelligent Investor by, Benjamin Graham

- The Warren Buffet Way by, Robert Hagstrom, Kenneth Fisher & Peter Lynch
- The Essay of Warren Buffet by, Warren Buffet.

I will be more than happy to share with you the two important learning that can serve as action points for you to start.

Firstly, all the books on personal finance teach us to **pay ourselves first.** Can you think of one resource that is equally distributed among all? It is neither money nor relationships. And it is not even hard to think about. I assume many of you may have surely have got the answer. Yes, it is none other than ***TIME.*** And the best thing about time is that it is scarce, and whatever is scarce is enormously valuable.

The first principle teaches us to pay a minimum of 20% of money we earn to ourselves first. Let us apply this principle to our topic of investments. You must invest at least 20% of your daily time to the topics mentioned in the list of investments, the results would be astounding and much greater than you can think of. It will first of all make your life purposeful and interesting. You will not regret getting up from the bed in the morning. Instead you will be waiting for the sunrise to jumpstart your day. And now apply the pay ourselves first principle. The very first hour or hours should be invested in yourselves i.e., ***pay yourself first.***

I am giving you an acronym that I found very useful in one of the books named The Miracle Morning, by Hal

Elrod. This can best fit your morning investment routine. The below mentioned visual will make it clear and easy to understand. Here S-Silence, A-affirmation, & V-visualization are for your mind. E-Exercise for your physique. R-Reading for your intellect and S-Scribing again to develop your intellectual faculties. This golden hour should be far from the reach of distractions like smart phone or any gadgets. You should be fully with yourselves and have some time for self – reflection daily. And if you can follow it for even a week, you will be amazed to see the positive changes in your life at all levels – physical, mental, emotional, spiritual, financial, and intellectual. It is worth doing.

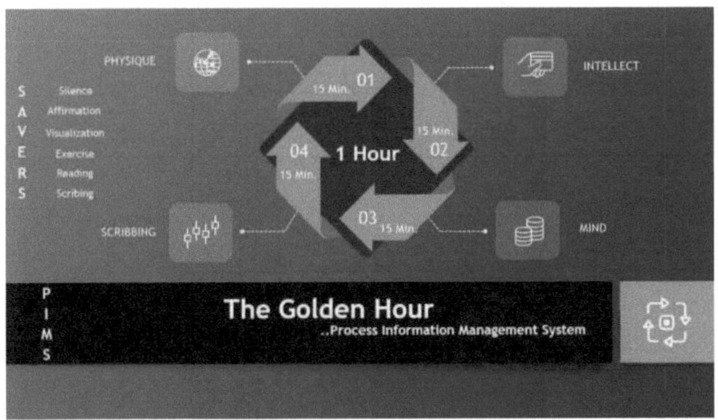

3. <u>Minimization</u>

It was funny to see how the economy was about to collapse

because people were only buying what they needed.

It was not funny at all but just for the sake of putting it, I mentioned the phrase the way I had read this somewhere during the quarantine era. What a time when the crude oil price in the history went down to negative on 21st April, 2020. This was something amazing to get to know how and why it happened especially for economics students and those who belong to the family of the stock market. I had to rub my eyes twice before believing the figure that I saw. I am sure you wouldn't have been able to first believe the figure. (-) $37.63 a barrel (source: The Hindu, updated 21st April, 16:28 IST). It was simply unbelievable and the reasons well explained by the mismatch of demand and supply.

I want you want to further know about the notorious crude oil price and volatility; you can further investigate about the dynamics of the oil industry. Before it starts to get boring, lets us get back to normal human lives and understand and learn *the art of minimization*.

You may also have seen people stocking up ration in an act of panic buying. Doesn't the phrase which is mentioned at the starting mean that all the years we have been spending money on the things that are non-essential, if not all but many of the things. These were the things that have been eating up our credit cards and destroying our liquidity. This non-essential or maximization style of living robs us of our psychological well-being in search of happiness. But we must have realized the worldly non-essential things seldom were able to bring happiness in times of crisis. Many would have struggled with personal cash reserve and for those who had lost their jobs, it would have been worse to live with credit card bills and impending doom languishing over their careers.

This reminds me of a very interesting quote by the master of investing, Warren Buffet again:

> "If you buy things that you don't need,
>
> you will soon sell things that you need"

Put in further simple words, it means the act of sacrifice of non-significant things over significant things. So, the learning here is to learn *the art of sacrifice*. Not very easy but not very tough either.

I can`t stop to mention here an extraordinary act of sacrifice so tough for anyone to navigate. This also resembles with one of the chapters on inspiration that teaches us to put our country first (You will later encounter in the book.) CM for Uttar Pradesh, Shri Yogi Adityanath deserves an standing ovation and a salute for his decision of serving his country at the cost of being absent in his father`s last rites . His father, late Anand Singh Bisht, then aged 89, died in Delhi on 20th April 2020.

May his soul rest in peace and I would urge all to observe a silence of at least a minute before proceeding further to pay a homage to his father.

Our country will always be obliged by the gift he has provided our country with in the likes of Shri Yogi Aditya Nath who has been devoting his life to the mankind.

Even at such a weak time, he continued with his meetings in support to India`s war against the Pandemic.

To conclude with, let us reinforce the *art of sacrifice*. One of the finest learnings during the pandemic.

4. Re-invention

I don`t think it will be wrong to say that our mother Earth re-invented herself and for the Earth day celebration on 22nd April 2020. It had so many achievements to boast about like the much better air quality index all around the world particularly Northern India, the clean water of the Ganges & Yamuna, improved climate conditions and what not.

This year`s Earth day observed was quite silent but a boon to the mother land otherwise with the pace with which we were going or harming, days were not far when we had to lockdown nations deliberately without any pandemic. Entire nations worldwide would have created a pandemic like situation if not this one.

This is on a broader level but what does reinvention mean on a more personal level? And can we really do so? If we don't re-invent, what could be the things that we might lose and regret?

This has been perhaps the best time to re-invent ourselves. Let us start by observing some examples who have re-invented themselves and gained and who couldn't and lost in the whirlpool of time.

I have taken examples that reign from the topmost personalities to the common man so that it is not only limited to books and the sake of book reading. It must become a much needed action point in your life.

Let us firstly start with none another than the Angry Young Man, Shri Amitabh Bachchan who was born on 11 October, 1942. He debuted with the film Saat Hindustani. It is a known fact that his voice was rejected twice by the All India Radio. But the more interesting fact is in the film industry he had his first income of around Rs.300 for voice over for narration in the film Bhuvan Shome.

His career is well-known to everyone but what we are looking at is how re-inventing brought him riches and also played an important part in his career. Keeping our focus on learning the *art of re-inventing*. To learn from such a legendary man is indeed worth your time.

Soon after his movies were not doing as splendid as it was expected, he decided to take a break from acting after his movie *"Khuda Gawah"*. *A step towards re-invention.* He started a company ABCL which couldn't do well. This move made him realize that he was born to act and would be more successful with his acting career rather than business.

And before I forget to tell you that prior to this he also tried his career at politics but soon after being surrounded by disputes he parted with his career in politics.

After returning to the acting career which was his another step to re-invention was as we all know his entry to the small screen which nobody would have ever thought of. Yes, a legendary man of silver screen coming to small screen i.e through *"Kaun Banega Corepati Show"*. And the rest is history as we all might know. Then he silenced all the critics about his old age with a dashing performance in *"Bbuddha... Hoga Terra Baap"*. He partnered with actors of all ages to do what he best does.

What we need to pay attention here is not his glam career but the way he has been re-inventing every time when it was the demand of the hour. The best piece to learn about his entire career is the ***art of re-invention,*** without shying away from opportunities. The other stars who have failed to re-invent themselves are well known to settle down early in their career with lack of stardom.

Secondly, let us move to more common platform from a glam life. Remember the time of demonetization with so much of apprehensions around it. Can you connect re-invention here?

Let me put it across, if it wouldn't have happened, and the Covid-19 pandemic had extended its wings before demonetization (which gave rise to adopting digital payments by the masses that was primarily a thing for tech-savvy educated masses earlier), things would have been much worse during the quarantine era. The re-invention of payment methods with the likes of Paytm, Google Pay beside many others, served a lot during the tough times.

We were even able to buy veggies, essentials and what not with just few taps on our mobile phones. The masses who adopted re-invention included a huge range right from big brands to small shopkeepers, stall veggie seller to big baskets, dairies to all the possible purchases. Tiniest of transactions worth Re.1 to Rs.100 to significant big amounts could be done through the wallets and digital payments which has helped a lot of people to survive during the tough times and also curb the spread of the pandemic by reduced visits to ATMs and exchange of any physical instruments of markets.

Those who couldn't re-invent themselves with the use of digital payments due to apprehensions and rumors of digital theft must have been left disheartened with their decisions.

Thirdly, in the professional world, those who were earlier anxious about online meets and virtual training session must have realized its importance. Even when we planned training sessions for our company during the lockdown times, it was a huge success with participation in each session booming with more than 50 in each session as compared to 10-15 earlier. And why not. It has several advantages over the traditional methods like:

1. The constraints of physical seating capacity is removed all together.
2. It is more economical rather than conducting physical meets or training sessions.
3. The ease of recording for further reference unlike physical meets wherein we need special equipment and arrangements to record.

It has significant various other benefits that you can explore on your own. Now what has been the thought process behind online learning is bound to change where physical attendance and learning has always been given preference.

Though online learning has been gaining grounds over the past few years. Let us understand more closely through a picture with some stats from a recent report by KPMG in India Research & Analysis.

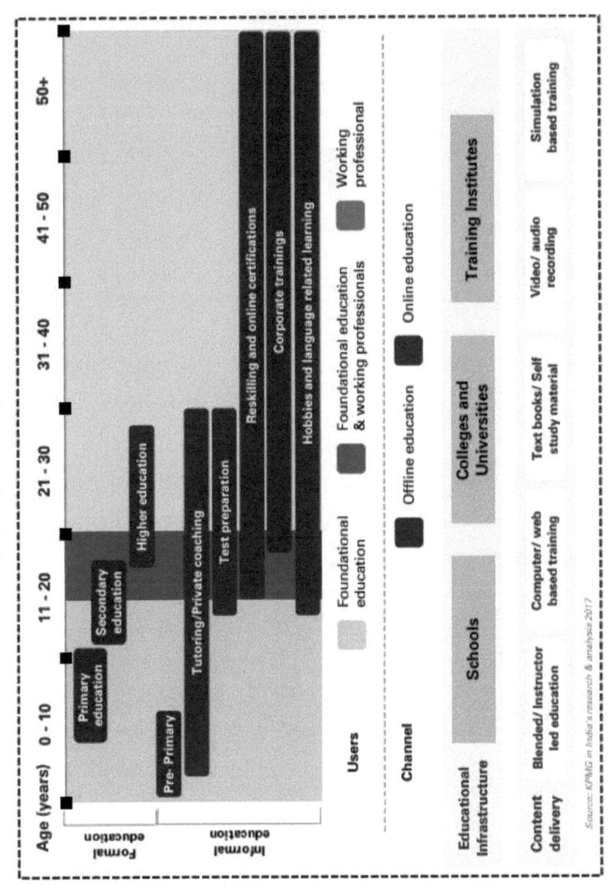

Source: KPMG in India Research & Analysis 2017

If you carefully go through the visual which presents very interesting facts about online education system in India, it is evident that it is yet to be integrated and streamlined with our core education system especially at school & college & Higher Education levels. Why not leverage the advantage of online presence in education rather than limiting online presence just for the sake of promotions and acquiring so called customers?

But it has its own challenges of content pricing, availability of employment opportunities and connectivity. Even with these challenges it is bound to outshine with its advantages of convenience, ease of concentrating at home, reduced travel time besides noteworthy others.

We at first have to understand and accept the fact that still students, parents, teachers, professionals and corporations are anxious about the online methodology. Though the tech companies have really done a great job as their core is invention and re-invention.

The problems in education sector is partly due to the outbreak of the pandemic, but more than the outbreak, it is the lack of ability to re-invent. We may not have thought the need yet, but this is a great reminder to land ourselves in the world of re-invention to bring back the gloss. The old methods need to make way for the new ones.

But I am concerned over the common masses who find it difficult and rather have trust issues. People don't accept the advantages or fail to abide by the law of nature. Specially the education system that needs a deep overhauling process to strengthen the roots. This is possible only when people start trusting and having faith on the re-invention process.

So, to conclude with whenever time demands, learn the *art of re-invention*. The quarantine era has been the best teacher of re-invention.

5. Graduating to be a Human

"How many disasters do we need to unite humanity?"
-Loesje

Are we graduated to be a human?

Perhaps the lock down during the quarantine era was a graduation session for all. Yet some failed drastically in the test. We have seen shameless acts of stone pelting at multiple places, abusive behavior towards doctors. What can be more drastic than these acts especially during such a critical spell?

On the other hand, there were many who graduated to be human with high flying and distinction marks.

An act of humanity where our Muslim brothers performed the last rites for an old woman who died, heroes who put their lives at risk to distribute food, families who gave rations to their tenants who were daily wage earners and the examples are endless.

Even few kids were very young who graduated to be human by donating their piggy bank savings in times of need for the PM CARES fund. There is no other country like India and never will be. That's for sure. And this kind of graduation degree to qualify as a human can be found in plenty in India. But I must praise the heroes world over who put their best foot forward for their respective nations.

Ask yourselves now, did you graduate to be a human? Or were you a silent observer? If you have not done your part still it is not too late. Pull up your socks and get the real qualification to have a high self-esteem and a sense of satisfaction that none of the pleasures and gratifications of the world can provide.

The state & the central government did and are still doing the best that they can do to support and provide relief. And I must ask all those who pass the buck to our government, if only government is supposed to do everything, then what are we supposed to do? I leave the answer to all the readers.

I will be more than Enlightened to get the answer to this question.

- *Impact of Covid`19 on Education*

-Specially crafted for students, teachers, principals and educators & life-long learners

Now comes the damage control times ahead and the *survival of the fittest.* Being optimistic enough let us explore the impacts and not only that, also we will look how can we make the most even in challenging situations and re-invent our thought process and methodologies towards education.

The impact of the pandemic knows no bounds. The everlasting impression in different spheres of life has been, I would say spectacular. Looking towards the positive side which has really been an act of courage and rare to be encouraging, yet there were strong sways in economical, psychological, socio-cultural, Environmental, Political, Geographical & Technological spheres of lives. Here I will try to bring about the sways in education and learning domain.

I will refer to a very strategic research conducted by Mindler Education pvt. Ltd. First of all a big thank you to the founder of Mindler, for bringing out such useful insights.

The immaculate research was conducted to understand the impact of COVID-19 pandemic on the decisions made by school students in Grades 11-12, regarding their higher education plans. Due to the unanticipated environments, students have been facing a dilemma about their respective career journeys. Given the timing of the lockdown in India, there has been a direct impact on school students; caused by postponement of board exams, entrance exams, standardized tests, delay in college admissions, confusion about admission dates and more. The research focused on understanding the impact on students and to hear student voices on this matter. It was conducted via an online survey from over 47,560 students across hundreds of schools in India. Of the students surveyed 56% of the respondents were girls and 44% were boys

While everyone was taken by surprise, none of us were prepared for such a situation. But on the brighter side it led to the transformation of the global higher education sector. All the educational institutes were speechless and have been facing challenging yet interesting time ahead.

First of all we are bound to see a new normal for higher education sector which will be revolutionized faster than ever. This will also pave the way for change in which the universities evaluate screen applications. Perhaps the most interesting turnaround will be how the decision to study abroad will see a drastic makeover. This also suggests that Indian Universities will see a massive surge in applications.

Has COVID-19 affected your career plans?

With the changing scenario, it is inevitable that students are reconsidering their initial career plans. The COVID-19 has forced the students to revisit their initial choices, and comprehend the viability of their decisions due to significant changes caused by delay in board examinations, postponement of entrance exams and confusion about admission dates. It is evident from the graph above, that out of the total number of students who participated in this survey around **63%** feel their career plans are being affected.

Has your choice of career domain been affected by the COVID-19 outbreak?

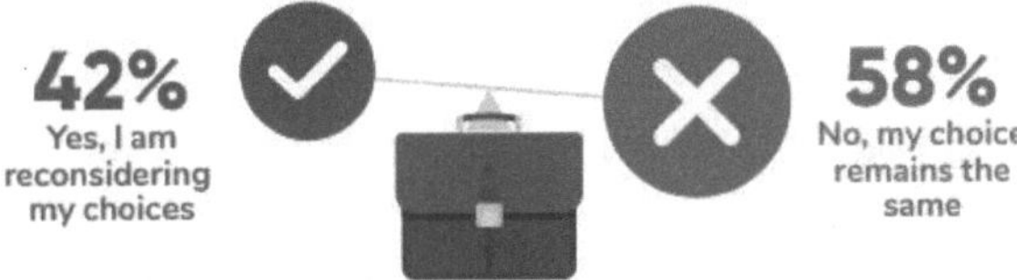

Given the postponement of board exams and entrance examinations which are the dominant routes to entry to colleges it is clear that a significant proportion of the students are reconsidering their choices. As per the study around **58%** of the students said their career domain choice remains the same while **42%** are reconsidering their decision. Students are also considering career backups so that they can have more options to choose from.

Moving on, if you see the below stats, majority of students feel the need to reconsider their initial career plans. The pandemic has forced them to revisit their initial choices and comprehend the viability of due to unexpected changes and delays in board and entrance examinations. This fact is reinforced further by the confusion of dates.

Now if we look at the impact on career domain around 42% of students said they are re-thinking about their career domain and are also considering career backup so that they have multiple options to choose from. While 58% still would prefer to go with the choices they had initially made.

Moving towards specially the entrance exams which see lakhs of students ever year to hover from their native places to renowned hubs of education. We see massive students rush to several parts of the country. Usually, the board exams and entrance tests are completed in a complete harmony with entrance exams coming in to the picture as soon as board exams see an end. But this year it has been quite different at large. Most of the students have struggled to cope up with mounting pressure. Majority of the students have been anxious about entrance exams and their preparation.

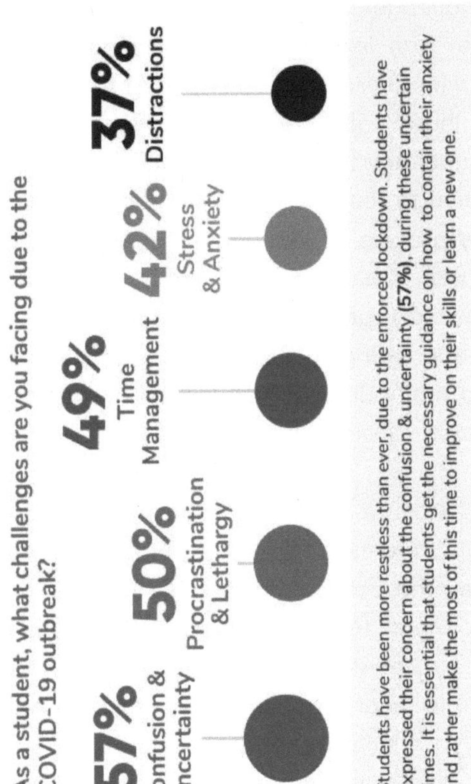

Some of the major challenges experiences by students (and others also) are:

1. Confusion & Uncertainty
2. Procrastination & Lethargy
3. Time Management
4. Stress & Anxiety
5. Distractions

These challenges are the indicators for educators where they can leverage the opportunity to help the students with these encounters. If students can well manage these with the help of their mentors and support functions like family, friends & relatives, they can unfailingly benefit from this opportunity to re-invent the process of learning. This will also give rise to new career options which they can explore. You as a student can get away from mundane ways of learning and being to experiment with your learning styles and methodology. You will find more on this in the chapters "Inside the mind" & learning how to learn.

One very interesting finding I came across in newspaper, *the Economic times (1st May2020)*. It said that academics from IIMs particularly Ahmedabad, Calcutta, Lucknow and Indore are revising this year's curriculum to incorporate learnings from the pandemic into nearly all subjects. These institutes are worth the praise as this was perhaps the first time ever, that academics have to tweak the courses in real-time to reflect the changing reality of the situation outside the campus. The broad areas on macroeconomics are to be covered like the Supreme court`s capping of Covid-19 testing to discuss price controls and infection transmission to include the idea of *externalities*. Investment in public health facilities to be discussed as a part of investment in public goods.

My area of interest would be to know how well these studies will fair in understanding of personal finance. Perhaps giving due importance to *Personal Financial*

Management will help the study more effectively. I strongly feel the method to be *inside out* first and then *outside in*. The broader level or the country and world live levels understanding will surely help, but it should also be on a much atomic level i.e. personal finance that are seldom taught. Combining these two studies would create a perfect blend of understanding.

These developments and others in the Education sector is giving a hint to the new normal in the post-Covid world.

In the upcoming paragraphs, I will also try to help to do the reverse engineering to get a good grasp of the COVID-19 by bringing to you its history and evolution, , prediction by Bill Gates, in 2015 & Remedies through one of his TED talks, the way to ***HEAL*** (learn about this principle in upcoming chapters) your knowledge about coronavirus. You will also be able to get to the answers to some of the most interesting questions related to the event like - How Does virus Work, How do vaccines work, Why is it dangerous, What has given rise to COVID`19, Replication Process, How significantly dangerous is it, What can you do? Practical Steps, and Future of COVID-19 and pandemics.

https://www.worldometers.info/coronavirus/#repro

How dangerous is the virus?

There are three parameters to understand in order to assess the magnitude of the risk posed by this novel coronavirus:

1. **Transmission Rate (Ro)** - number of newly infected people from a single case
2. **Case Fatality Rate (CFR)** - percent of cases that result in death
3. **Determine** whether asymptomatic transmission is possible

How contagious is the Wuhan Coronavirus? (Ro)

The attack rate or transmissibility (how rapidly the disease spreads) of a virus is indicated by its reproductive number (Ro, pronounced R-nought or r-zero), which represents the average number of people to which a single infected person will transmit the virus. WHO's estimated (on Jan. 23) Ro to be between 1.4 and 2.5. Other studies have estimated a Ro between 3.6 and 4.0, and between 2.24 to 3.58. Preliminary studies had estimated Ro to be between 1.5 and 3.5. An outbreak with a reproductive number of below 1 will gradually disappear.

For comparison, the Ro for the common flu is 1.3 and for SARS it was 2.0

Fatality Rate (case fatality ratio or CFR) of the Wuhan Coronavirus.

The novel coronavirus case fatality rate has been estimated at around 2%, in the WHO press conference held on January 29, 2020. However, it noted that, without knowing how many were infected, it was too early to be able to put a percentage on the mortality rate figure. A prior estimate had put that number at 3%. Fatality rate can change as a virus can mutate, according to epidemiologists. For comparison, the case fatality rate for SARS was 10%, and for MERS 34%.

Incubation Period (how long it takes for symptoms to appear)

Symptoms of COVID-19 may appear in as few as 2 days or as long as 14 (estimated ranges vary from 2-10 days, 2-14 days, and 10-14 days, see details), during which the virus is contagious, but the patient does not display any symptom (asymptomatic transmission).

Age and conditions of Coronavirus cases

According to early estimates by China's National Health Commission (NHC), about 80% of those who died were over the age of 60 and 75% of them had pre-existing health conditions such as cardiovascular diseases and diabetes. According to the WHO Situation Report no. 7 issued on Jan. 27:

The median age of cases detected outside of China is 45 years, ranging from 2 to 74 years. 71% of cases were male. A study of 138 hospitalized patients with NCIP found that the median age was 56 years (interquartile range, 42-68; range, 22-92 years) and 75 (54.3%) were men.

The WHO, in its Myth busters FAQs, addresses the question: "Does the new coronavirus affect older people, or are younger people also susceptible?" by answering that:

People of all ages can be infected by the novel coronavirus COVID-19.
Older people, and people with pre-existing medical conditions (such as asthma, diabetes, heart disease) appear to be more vulnerable to becoming severely ill with the virus. Patient who died in the Philippines was a 44-year old male. The patient who died in the Philippines on February 2, in what was the first death occurring outside of China, was a 44-year-old Chinese man from Wuhan who was admitted on Jan. 25 after experiencing fever, cough, and sore throat, before developing severe pneumonia. In the last few days, “the patient was stable and showed signs of improvement, however, the condition of the patient deteriorated within his last 24 hours resulting in his demise." according to the Philippine Department of Health.

Serious Cases of 30-year-old patients in France

As of Jan. 29, according to French authorities, the conditions of the two earliest Paris cases had worsened and the patients were being treated in intensive care, according to French authorities. The patients have been described as a young couple aged 30 and 31 years old, both Chinese citizens from Wuhan who were asymptomatic when they arrived in Paris on January 18.

The NHC reported the details of the first 17 deaths up to 24 pm on January 22, 2020. The deaths included 13 males and 4 females. The median age of the deaths was 75 (range 48-89) years.

WHO Risk Assessment: Global Emergency

On January 30, the World Health Organization declared the coronavirus outbreak a Global Public Health Emergency.

Comparisons:

Every year an estimated 290,000 to 650,000 people die in the world due to complications from seasonal influenza (flu) viruses. This figure corresponds to 795 to 1,781 deaths per day due to the seasonal flu.

SARS (November 2002 to July 2003): was a coronavirus that originated from Beijing, China, spread to 29 countries, and resulted in 8,096 people infected with 774 deaths (fatality rate of 9.6%). Considering that SARS ended up infecting 5,237 people in mainland China, Wuhan Coronavirus surpassed SARS on January 29, 2020, when Chinese officials confirmed 5,974 cases of the novel coronavirus (2019-nCoV). One day later, on January 30, 2020 the novel coronavirus cases surpassed even the 8,096 cases worldwide which were the final SARS count in 2003.

MERS (in 2012) killed 858 people out of the 2,494 infected (fatality rate of 34.4%).

Bill Gates Prediction, 2015

Before proceeding further, let us first take responsibility to save ourselves from ***Dogmatization,*** which simply means confusion of facts with opinions. You may also have come across the rumormongers. So, whatever you have read and heard about the most *novel* and fascinating term since December 2019, i.e., CORONA VIRUS or better named as COVID-19, mostly has been opinions. Let me reveal and share information and not my opinion. For this information, you must first know about the source where I got to know such critical information. Let us first try to quickly understand their credentials before you deep dive on a journey that has been history in the making since its inception.

The first one, Mr. Bill Gates, and I am sure you won't demand any credentials for him.

The second one is a global health expert, Alanna Shaikh. She is a global health consultant and executive coach who specialize in individual, organizational, and systemic resilience. She holds a bachelor's degree from Georgetown University and a master's degree in public health from Boston University. She has lived in seven countries and is the author of- "What's Killing Us: A Practical Guide to Understanding Our Biggest Global Health Problems." Recent article publications include an article on global health security in Britain's Daily Telegraph newspaper and an essay in the Annual Review of Comparative and International Education. She blogs on coaching and personal resilience at

www.thisworldneedsbrave.com. This talk was given at a TEDx event using the TED.

Are we ready now? Yes, we are.

Today I am reminded of one of the TED talks that were given by Bill Gates in 2015 regarding the next outbreak and how we were not ready for it. Let me share some interesting findings from that conference.

He started by saying that when he was a child, his biggest fear was Nuclear war. But today the greatest risk of global catastrophe doesn't look like the picture of Nuclear war. Instead, it looked like the picture that we have seen as the Coronavirus. He further emphasized that if anything kills over 10 million people over the next few decades, it was most likely to be a highly infectious virus rather than a war. I still wonder how come he knew in advance. It was absolutely bang on. My God. Such a prediction with so much precision.

He clearly says that we are not ready for the next epidemic. The countries all over the world have invested a lot on war weapons. But seldom they have invested in which was and still required.

He reminded us of the horrific global outbreak of Ebola in 2014, thanks to thousands of selfless health workers -- plus, frankly, thanks to some very good luck. In his words – "the problem wasn't that the system didn't work well enough, the problem was that we didn't have a system at all."

According to Mr. Gates, the key missing pieces were:

1. We didn't have a group of epidemiologists ready to go, who would have gone, to see what the disease was, see how far it had spread.
2. The case reports came in on paper. It was much delayed before they were put online, and they were extremely inaccurate.
3. We didn't have a medical team ready to go.
4. We didn't have a way of preparing people.
5. Now, Médecins Sans Frontières did a great job orchestrating volunteers.
6. There was no one there to look at treatment approaches, diagnostics, and to figure out what tools should be used.

7. The things listed here were considered global failure. The WHO is funded to monitor epidemics, but not to do these things he talked about.

I remember the strongest convincing lines by him, "The failure to prepare could allow the next epidemic," and that is exactly what has happened to be dramatically more devastating than Ebola.

Let's also look at the progression of Ebola then where about 10,000 people died, and nearly all were in the three West African countries.

There were three reasons why it didn't spread more.

1. The first was that there was a lot of heroic work by the health workers. They found the people, and they prevented more infections.

2. The second is the nature of the virus. And, by the time they were contagious; most people were so sick that they were bedridden. Additionally, Ebola does not spread through the air.

3. Third, it didn't get into many urban areas. And that was just luck. If it had gotten into a lot of more urban areas, the case numbers would have been much larger. So next time, we might not be so lucky. And that has exactly been the case where countries around the world struggled and are still struggling.

He mentioned that we can have a virus where people feel well enough while they're infectious that they get on a plane or they go to a market. This is precisely what has been happening with COVID-19.

The source of the virus could be a natural epidemic like Ebola, or it could be bioterrorism.
So, there are things that have literally made things thousand times worse. In fact, he also showed us a model of a virus spread through the air like the Spanish Flu back in 1918. So, here's what would happen:
It would spread throughout the world very, very quickly. And you can see over 30 million people died from that epidemic. So, this is a serious problem. We should be concerned.

But in fact, we can build an excellent response system. We have the benefits of all the science and technology that we talk about here. We've got cell phones to get information from the public and get information out to them. We have satellite maps where we can see where people are and where they're moving.

He strongly believes that we have advances in biology that should dramatically change the turnaround time to look at a pathogen and be able to make drugs and vaccines that fit for that pathogen. So, we can have tools, but those tools need to be put into an overall global health system. And we need preparedness. The best lessons, he thinks, on how to get prepared are again, what we do for war.

For soldiers, we have full-time, waiting to go. We have reserves that can scale us up to large numbers. NATO has a mobile unit that can deploy very rapidly. NATO does a lot of war games to check, are people well trained? Do they understand about fuel and logistics and the same radio frequencies? So, they are absolutely ready to go. So those are the kinds of things we need to do to deal with an epidemic.

What are the key pieces, according to him?

First, we need strong health systems in poor countries, where mothers can give birth safely kids can get all their vaccines. This is because, that's where we'll see the outbreak very early on.

Second, we need a medical reserve corps: lots of people who've got the training and background who are ready to go, with the expertise. And then we need to pair those medical people with the military taking advantage of the military's ability to move fast, do logistics and secure areas. We need to do simulations, germ games not war games, so that we can see where the holes are. The last time a germ game was done in the United States was back in 2001, and it didn't go so well. So far, the score is germs: 1, people: 0.

Finally, we need lots of advanced R&D in areas of vaccines and diagnostics. There are some big breakthroughs, like the Adeno-associated virus, that could work very, very quickly. Now he also told us that he doesn't have an exact budget for what this would cost, but he is quite sure it's very modest compared to the potential harm.

The World Bank estimates that if we have a worldwide flu epidemic, global wealth will go down by over three trillion dollars, and we'd have millions and millions of deaths. These investments offer significant benefits beyond just being ready for the epidemic. The primary healthcare, the R&D, those things would reduce global health equity and make the world more just as well as safer. So, he thinks this should absolutely be a priority. There's no need to panic. We don't have to hoard cans of spaghetti or go down into the basement. But we need to get going because time is not on our side. In fact, if there's one positive thing that can come out of the Ebola epidemic, it's that it can serve as an early warning, a wake-up call, to get ready. If we start now, we can be ready for the next epidemic.

So, if Ebola was not strong enough, we now have the COVID-19 teaching us again, and if we don't pull up our socks now, there would be another epidemic much calamitous than ever before.

How Viruses Work

This discussion glides us to the CORONA VIRUS now. Allan Sheikh has nicely explained. Let me bring forth the findings. But before reading the words let us educate ourselves with critical pieces of working of virus and the working of vaccines to cure it. This has been very nicely explained by again a niche platform for learning, TED ed.

(https://www.youtube.com/watch?v=xjcsrU-ZmgY/ https://www.ted.com/talks/ben_longdon_how_do_viruses_jump_from_animals_to_humans/transcript)

As E.Q. Wilson has put in, "The variety of genes in viruses exceeds that in all of the rest of life combined." So how can pathogens from one species infect another, and what makes host jumps so dangerous?

Viruses are a type of organic parasite infecting nearly all forms of life. To survive and reproduce, they must move through three stages:

1. Contact with a susceptible host
2. Infection and replication
3. Transmission to other individuals.

As an example, let's look at human influenza. First, the flu virus encounters a new host and makes its way into their respiratory tract. This isn't so difficult, but to survive in this new body, the virus must mount a successful infection before it's caught and broken down by an immune response. To accomplish this task,
viruses have evolved specific interactions with their host species. Human flu viruses are covered in proteins adapted to bind with matching receptors on human respiratory cells.

Once inside a cell, the virus employs additional adaptations to hijack the host cell's reproductive machinery and replicate its own genetic material. Now the virus only needs to suppress or evade the host's immune system long enough to replicate to sufficient levels and infect more cells. At this point, the flu can be passed on to its next victim via any transmission of infected bodily fluid.

However, this simple sneeze also brings the virus in contact with pets, plants, or even your lunch. Viruses are constantly encountering new species and attempting to infect them. More often than not, this ends in failure. In most cases, the genetic dissimilarity between the two hosts is too great. For a virus adapted to infect humans, a lettuce cell would be a foreign and inhospitable landscape. But there are a staggering number of viruses circulating in the environment, all with the potential to encounter new hosts. And because viruses rapidly reproduce by the millions, they can quickly develop random mutations.

Most mutations will have no effect, or even prove detrimental; but a small proportion may enable the pathogen to better infect a new species. The odds of winning this destructive genetic lottery increase over time, or if the new species is closely related to the virus' usual host. For a virus adapted to another mammal, infecting a human might just take a few lucky mutations. And a virus adapted to chimpanzees, one of our closest genetic relatives, might barely require any changes at all. It takes more than time and genetic similarity for a host jump to be successful.

Some viruses come equipped to easily infect a new host's cells but are then unable to evade an immune response. Others might have a difficult time transmitting to new hosts. For example, they might make the host's blood contagious, but not their saliva. However, once a host jump reaches the transmission stage, the virus becomes much more dangerous. Now gestating within two hosts, the pathogen has twice the odds of mutating into a more successful virus. And each new host increases the potential for a full-blown epidemic.

Virologists are constantly looking for mutations that might make viruses such as influenza more likely to jump. However, predicting the next potential epidemic is a major challenge. There's a huge diversity of viruses that we're only just beginning to uncover. Researchers are tirelessly studying the biology of these pathogens. And by monitoring populations to quickly identify new outbreaks, they can develop vaccines and containment protocols to stop these deadly diseases.

How Vaccine Works

https://www.youtube.com/redirect?event=video_description&v=rb7TVW77ZCs&q=http%3A%2F%2Fed.ted.com%2Flessons%2Fhow-do-vaccines-work-kelwalin-dhanasarnsombut&redir_token=lJMooX1o6hQKYlmKXYWjBJuAgCZ8MTU4NDc4ODc1MkAxNTg0NzAyMzUy

Let us now also understand how vaccines work before diving in detail for the COVID-19.Also let us look at how vaccines work.

To understand how vaccines function, we need to know how the immune system defends us against contagious diseases in the first place. When foreign microbes invade us, the immune system triggers a series of responses in an attempt to identify and remove them from our bodies. The signs that this immune response is working are the coughing, sneezing, inflammation and fever we experience, which work to trap, deter and rid the body of threatening things, like bacteria.

These innate immune responses also trigger our second line of defense, called adaptive immunity. Special cells called B cells and T cells are recruited to fight microbes, and also record information about them, creating a memory of what the invaders look like, and how best to fight them. This know-how becomes handy if the same pathogen invades the body again. But despite this smart response, there's still a risk involved. The body takes time to learn how to respond to pathogens and to build up these defenses. And even then, if a body is too weak or young to fight back when it's invaded, it might face very serious risk if the pathogen is particularly severe.

But what if we could prepare the body's immune response, readying it before someone even got ill? This is where vaccines come in. Using the same principles that the body uses to defend itself, scientists use vaccines to trigger the body's adaptive immune system, without exposing humans to the full-strength disease. This has resulted in many vaccines, each work uniquely and are separated into many different types.

First, we have **live attenuated vaccines**. These are made of the pathogen itself but a much weaker and tamer version. Next, we have **inactive vaccines**, in which the pathogens have been killed. The weakening and inactivation in both types of vaccine ensures that pathogens don't develop into the full-blown disease. But just like a disease, they trigger an immune response, teaching the body to recognize an attack by making a profile of pathogens in preparation. The downside is that live attenuated vaccines can be difficult to make, and because they're live and quite powerful, people with weaker immune systems can't have them, while inactive vaccines don't create long-lasting immunity.

Another type, the **subunit vaccine**, is only made from one part of the pathogen, called an antigen, the ingredient that actually triggers the immune response. By even further isolating specific components of antigens, like proteins or polysaccharides, these vaccines can prompt specific responses. Scientists are now building a whole new range of vaccines called **DNA vaccines**. For this variety, they isolate the very genes that make the specific antigens the body needs to trigger its immune response to specific pathogens.

When injected into the human body, those genes instruct cells in the body to make the antigens. This causes a stronger immune response, and prepares the body for any future threats, and because the vaccine only includes specific genetic material, it doesn't contain any other ingredients from the rest of the pathogen that could develop into the disease and harm the patient. If these vaccines become a success, we might be able to build more effective treatments for invasive pathogens in the years to come. Just like Edward Jenner's amazing discovery spurred on modern medicine all those decades ago, continuing the development of vaccines might even allow us to treat diseases like HIV, malaria, or Ebola, one day.

Allan Sheikh, Health Expert`s View on COVID-19

She has worked in global-health journalism and written about global health and bio-security for newspapers and web outlets, and she had published a book a few years back about the major global health threats that we'll be facing as a planet. She has also supported and led epidemiological efforts that range from evaluating Ebola treatment centers to looking at transmission of tuberculosis in health facilities and doing avian influenza preparedness.

She has a master's degree in International Health. She is not a physician. She is not a nurse. Her specialty isn't patient care or taking care of individual people. Her specialty is looking at populations and health systems - what happens when diseases move on the large level. According to her, if we're ranking sources of global-health expertise on a scale of 1 to 10 -1 is some random person ranting on Facebook, and 10 is the World Health Organization - say you can probably put her at like a 7 or an 8. So, please keep that in mind as you read through. She starts with the basics here because I think that's gotten lost in some of the NOISE, about which you have read earlier/or will read in the chapters around COVID-19.

COVID-19 is a coronavirus, and coronaviruses are a specific subset of virus, and they have some unique characteristics as viruses. They use RNA instead of DNA as their genetic material, and they're covered in spikes on the surface of the virus, and they use these spikes to invade immune cells. These spikes are the corona in coronavirus. COVID-19 is known as a novel coronavirus because, until December, we'd only heard of six coronaviruses. COVID-19 is the seventh.
It's new to us, it just had its gene sequencing, it just got its name - that's why it's novel. If you remember SARS - severe acute respiratory syndrome - or MERS - Middle East respiratory syndrome, those were coronaviruses, and they're both caused respiratory syndromes because that's what coronaviruses do. They go for your lungs. Don't make you puke, they don't make you bleed from the eyeballs, they don't make you hemorrhage, they head for your lungs. COVID-19 is no different. It causes a range of respiratory symptoms that go from stuff like a dry cough and a fever all the way out to fatal viral pneumonia. And that range of symptoms is one of the reasons.

It's actually been so hard to track this outbreak. Plenty of people get COVID-19, but so gently, their symptoms are so mild that they don't even go to a health care provider. They don't register in the system. Children, in particular, have it very easy with COVID-19, which is something we should all be grateful for. Coronaviruses are zoonotic, which means that they transmit from animals to people. Some coronaviruses, like COVID-19, also transmit person to person. The person-to-person ones travel faster and travel farther, just like COVID-19.

Zoonotic illnesses are really hard to get rid of because they have an animal reservoir. One example is avian influenza, where we can abolish it in farmed animals, in turkeys, in ducks, but it keeps coming back every year because it's brought to us by wild birds. You don't hear a lot about it because avian influenza doesn't transmit from person to person, but we have outbreaks in poultry farms every year all over the world. COVID-19 most likely skipped from animals into people at a wild animal market in Wuhan, China.

Now, let’s get the less basic parts. This is not the last major outbreak we're ever going to see. There's going to be more outbreaks, and there's going to be more epidemics or pandemics. That's not a maybe; that's a given. And it's a result of the way that we, as human beings, are interacting with our planet. Human choices are driving us into a position where we're going to see more outbreaks. Part of that is about climate change and the way a warming climate makes the world more hospitable to viruses and bacteria.

But it's also about the way we're pushing into the last wild spaces on our planet. When we burn and plow the Amazon rain forest so that we can have cheap land for ranching, when the last of the African bush gets converted into farms, when wild animals in China are hunted to extinction, human beings come into contact with wildlife populations that they've never come into contact with before, and those populations have new kinds of diseases, bacteria, viruses - stuff we're not ready for. Bats, in particular, have a knack for hosting illnesses that can infect people.

But they're not the only animals that do it. So, as long as we keep making our remote places less remote, the outbreaks are going to keep coming. We can't stop the outbreaks with quarantine or travel restrictions. That's everybody's first impulse: Let's stop the people from moving, let's stop this outbreak from happening. But the fact is it's really hard to get a good quarantine in place. It's really hard to set up travel restrictions. Even the countries that have made serious investments in public health, like the US and South Korea, can't get that kind of restriction in place fast enough to actually stop an outbreak instantly.

There are logistical reasons for that, and there are medical reasons. If you look at COVID-19, right now, it's seems like it have a period where you're infected and show no symptoms that's as long as 24 days. So, people are walking around with this virus showing no signs. They're not going to get quarantined. Nobody knows they need quarantining. There are also some real costs to quarantine and to travel restrictions. Humans are social animals, and they resist when you try to hold them into place and when you try to separate them. We saw in the Ebola outbreak that as soon as you put a quarantine in place,

people start trying to evade it. Individual patients, if they know there's a strict quarantine protocol, may not go for health care because they're afraid of the medical system, or they can't afford health care, and they don't want to be separated from their family and friends. Politicians, government officials, when they know they're going to get quarantined, if they talk about outbreaks and cases, may conceal real information for fear of triggering a quarantine protocol. And, of course, these kinds of evasions and dishonesty are exactly what make it so difficult to track a disease outbreak.

We can get better at quarantines and travel restrictions, and we should. But they're not our only option, and they're not our best option for dealing with these situations. The real way for the long haul to make outbreaks less serious is to build the global health system to support core health-care functions in every country in the world so that all countries, even poor ones, are able to rapidly identify and treat new infectious diseases as they emerge.

China's taken a lot of criticism for its response to COVID-19. But the fact is what if COVID-19 had emerged in Chad, which has 3.5 doctors for every 100,000 people? What if it had emerged in the Democratic Republic of Congo, which just released its last Ebola patient from treatment? The truth is countries like this don't have the resources to respond to an infectious disease, not to treat people and not to report on it fast enough to help the rest of the world. She led an evaluation of Ebola treatment centers in Sierra Leone. And the fact is that local doctors in Sierra Leone identified the Ebola crisis very quickly.

First, as a dangerous and contagious hemorrhagic virus and then as Ebola itself. But having identified it, they didn't have the resources to respond. They didn't have enough doctors or hospital beds, and they didn't have enough information about how to treat Ebola or how to implement infection control.

Eleven doctors died in Sierra Leone of Ebola. The country only had 120 when the crisis started. In contrast, Dallas Baylor Medical Center has more than 1,000 physicians on staff. These are the kinds of inequities that kill people. First, they kill the poor people when the outbreaks start, and then they kill people all over the world when the outbreaks spread.

If we really want to slow down these outbreaks and minimize their impact, we need to make sure that every country in the world has the capacity to identify new diseases, treat them, and report about them so they can share information.

COVID-19 is going to be a huge burden on health systems. She doesn`t talk about death rates in this talk because, frankly, nobody can agree on the COVID-19 death rates right now. But one number we can agree on is that about 20% of people infected with COVID-19 are going to need hospitalization. The US medical system can just barely cope with that. But what's going to happen in Mexico? COVID-19 has also revealed some real weaknesses in our global health supply chains. Just-in-time ordering LEAN systems is great when things are going well, but in a time of crisis, what it means is we don't have any reserves. If a hospital or a country runs out of face masks or personal protective equipment, there's no big warehouse full of boxes that we can go to get more. You have to order more from the supplier, wait for them to produce it, and you have to wait for them to ship it, generally, from China. That's a time lag at a time when it's most important to move quickly. If we'd been perfectly prepared for COVID-19, China would have identified the outbreak faster. They would have been ready to provide care to infected people without having to build new buildings.

They should have shared honest information with citizens so that we didn't see these crazy rumors spreading on social media in China. And they should have shared information with global health authorities so that they could start reporting to national health systems and getting ready for the time when the virus spread. National health systems would then have been able to stockpile the protective equipment they needed and train health care providers on treatment and infection control. We'd have science-based protocols for what to do when things happen, like cruise ships have infected patients.

And we'd have real information going out to people everywhere, so we wouldn't see embarrassing, shameful incidents as xenophobia, like Asian-looking people getting attacked on the streets in Philadelphia. But even with all that in place, we would still have outbreaks.

The choices we're making about how we occupy this planet make that inevitable. As far as we have an expert consensus on COVID-19, it's this here in the US and globally, it's going to get worse before it gets better. We're seeing cases of human transmission that aren't from returning travel, that are just happening in the community. And we're seeing people infected with COVID-19 when we don't even know where the infection came from. Those are signs of an outbreak that's getting worse, not an outbreak that's under control. It's depressing, but it's not surprising. Global health experts, when they talk about the scenario of new viruses, this is one of the scenarios that they look at. We all hoped we'd get off easy.

But when experts talk about viral planning, this is the kind of situation and the way they expect the virus to move. She closed the talk with some personal advice.

1. Wash your hands! Wash your hands a lot! We know that you already wash your hands a lot because you're not disgusting. But wash your hands even more.

2. Set up cues and routines in your life to get you to wash your hands. Wash your hands every time you enter and leave a building. Wash your hands when you go in and come out of a meeting. Get rituals there based around hand washing.

3. Sanitize your phone. You touch that phone with your dirty, unwashed hands all the time. We all know you take it into the bathroom with you. So, sanitize your phone and consider not using it as often in public.

4. Don't touch your face. Don't rub your eyes. Don't bite your fingernails.

5. Don't wear a face mask. Yes, you read it right. Face masks are for sick people and health care providers. If you're sick, your face mask holds in all your coughing and sneezing and protects the people around you. And, if you're a health care provider, your face mask is one tool in a set of tools called personal protective equipment, that you're trained to use so you can give patient care and not get sick yourself. If you're a regular, healthy person wearing a face mask, it's just making your face sweaty. Leave the face masks in stores for the doctors and the nurses and the sick people.

6. If you think you have symptoms of COVID-19, stay home, call your doctor for advice. If you're diagnosed with COVID-19, remember, it's generally very mild.

7. And if you're a smoker, right now is the best possible time to quit smoking. I mean, if you're a smoker, right now is always the best possible time to quit smoking. But if you're a smoker

> and you're worried about COVID-19, I guarantee that quitting is absolutely the best thing you can do to protect yourself from the worst impacts of COVID-19.

COVID-19 is scary stuff at a time when pretty much all of our news feels like scary stuff. And there are a lot of bad but appealing options for dealing with it: panic, xenophobia, agoraphobia, authoritarianism, oversimplified lies that make us think that hate and fury and loneliness are the solution to outbreaks. But they're not, they just make us less prepared.

There's also a boring but useful set of options that we can use in response to outbreaks, things like improving health care, here and everywhere; investing in health infrastructure and disease surveillance so that we know when the new diseases come; building health systems all over the world; looking at strengthening our supply chains so they're ready for emergencies; and better education, so we're capable of talking about disease outbreaks and the mathematics of risk without just blind panic. We need to be guided by equity here because in this situation, like so many, equity is actually in our own self-interest.

Chapter 3: HEAL your Learning.

Before the outbreak, our world was entirely different. While I was trying to write around 11:25 PM in the night on January 25, 2020, just a few hours before the 71st Republic day, I was excited to watch the morning news. And this year, it was extraordinary for me. The school that served as a heaven for me when I was studying from 2007-2009, yes, my *heaven* is to participate in the Republic Day celebration, and I can`t wait for the morning, goose bumps all over and I couldn't stop sharing this with my friends and family.

Amid all the negative situations; the CAA protests, JNU uproar, fire in Delhi wood factory in Aya Nagar, where seven firefighter trucks are struggling, and I wonder how we can have so many recent incidents of fire. Moreover, the Shaheen Bagh incident makes me go crazy and berserk. How can a ten-year-old speak such evil? Corona Virus in China was spreading, not significantly enough apart from China that could pose a threat to the world, and people were kept in quarantine.

Padma Awardee list was announced on the Republic Day eve that included many of my favorites, whose name I can`t stop myself from taking; Late Arun Jaitley for public affairs, M.C Mary Kom for sports, Muzzaffar Hussain Baig for public affairs, P.V Sindhu, Ekta

Kapoor & Karan Johar in the field of Sports, Arts and many more.

Ok, so you are wondering why I am discussing this. It`s ok to think, and I do understand. So yes, you can well imagine now that questions keep popping up in your head, which I refer to as *NOISE.* You will know about this term more clearly later on.

I have realized all my growing years that I was reading and writing to respond and form an opinion rather than understanding and extracting the real meaning and the learning behind it. I was collecting information. You are the lucky ones that you are enjoying the *early bird discount*; I was not fortunate enough to avail of this facility. I was among the thinkers that didn't board this journey and could board later on for sure after paying the *price*. I learned it the hard way, but in India, we have a saying, *"Der aaye dusurst aaye"- Better late than never.*

The thing to understand here is to realize that we have given control of our thoughts to our external factors. Is this correct? So, let us begin our journey by asking ourselves to which team do we belong? Are you in the group that is driven by the external environment or the one who exercises your power and are least affected by the external factors? The clearer we are with this fact, the more helpful it will be for you to grow. Think about when you decide to act. Is it you who decide, or are your decisions driven by external stimuli? This answer to this question will help you to make your journey easier. So, I recommend you all to give it a deep and insightful thought before beginning this journey.

Let me help you here and take your last week. Ask yourself questions like:

1. How have the previous seven days unfolded in your life? (Alternatively, you may also opt to take one month, or a year or any term. For ease of the purpose it serves, I have just taken seven days)
2. Were you able to do what you decided before the start of the week? Or you didn't decide anything at all for the week!
3. Have you been happy in the last seven days?
4. Have you been stressed in the last seven days?

The first step towards learning starts from the first alphabet of English i.e., so you already thought of "A", right?

Before formulating the solutions in your mind, you must accept the fact that you often do express the solutions and form opinions and conclusions much before it concludes. It doesn't allow you to learn. Instead, you develop a layer that doesn't let you do the learning to hook or stick to your mind.

And whenever that layer is troubled by external factors, all the learning, and to rephrase *learning* as *opinions,* are easily shaken because the learning is not as firm as it should be. So, the beliefs you form during the process of learning are mistaken as learning by you.

Let us take the plunge back to history, don't worry about the *price* to travel, remember I told you I am not a money- person but yes I will charge a *price* for this, and you have to *pay* me later on when you reach your destinations. This step will help you in decoding the secret to actual learning without forming opinions as the learning hooks and sticks to your mind effortlessly.

Source:
http://www.todayifoundout.com/index.php/2013/09/the-origin-of-the-english-alphabet/

Station *history* Boarded:
The moment you thought about the alphabet A when I told you about the first alphabet of English, that was the moment when you have to tell your mind, "O my babes (mind); I own you, and you have to take my orders, and I order you that before thinking and wandering about the alphabet A, tell me how did the alphabet A come into being. Tell me the origin and the background". Come on, start working for me." So, my mind begins to attract real answers. Here`s what my mind got for me:

The modern English alphabet was not a one-time discovery/invention. It was a result and outcome of hundreds of years, several languages, and a variety of scholars, missionaries, and conquerors. It is considered as one of the most challenging languages to master due to incredible inconsistencies in the language.

Origins of Alphabetic Writing
Dating back nearly four thousand years, early alphabetic writing, relied on simple lines to represent spoken sounds as opposed to other old forms of writing like cuneiform (which employed the use of different wedge shapes) or hieroglyphics (which primarily used pictographic symbols). Scholars attribute its origin to a little known Proto-Sinaitic, the

Semitic form of writing developed in Egypt between 1800 and 1900 BC.

Building on this ancient foundation, the first widely used alphabet was developed by the Phoenicians about seven hundred years later. Consisting of 22 letters, all consonants, this Semitic language became used throughout the Mediterranean, including in the Levant, the Iberian Peninsula, North Africa, and southern Europe.

The Greeks built on the Phoenician alphabet by adding vowels sometime around 750 BC. Considered the first true alphabet, it was later appropriated by the Latins (then to become the Romans) who combined it with notable Etruscan characters, including the letters "F" and "S." Although ancient Latin omitted G, J, V (or U)*, W, Y, and Z, by about the third century, the Roman alphabet looked very similar to our modern English, containing every letter except J, U (or V)* and W.

(*V and U have a complicated shared history. Both were used throughout the Middle Ages, although they were considered a single letter until quite recently.)

Old English

The history of writing in Britain begins with the Anglo-Saxons in the fifth century AD. With ties to Scandinavia and other North Seas cultures, ancient Anglo-Saxon writing, called futhorc, was a runic language. Flexible, new runes were routinely added such that, although it first appeared in England with 26 characters, by the time of its demise (by the 11th century AD), it had 33.

In the seventh century AD, the Latin alphabet introduced by Christian missionaries had begun to take hold. By 1011, a formal list of the Old English alphabet was made and included all of our present letters except J, U (or V)* and W. The ampersand and five uniquely English letters, designated ond, wynn, thorn, eth and ash, were included.

Middle English

Shortly after the Old English alphabet was first set down, the Normans invaded (1066 AD). English as a language was relegated primarily to the low born, with the nobility, clergy and scholars speaking or writing in Norman or Latin.

By the 13th century when, writing in English began to become more prominent again, the language reflected two centuries of Norman rule. The Old English letters thorn, and eth were replaced by "th"; wynn eventually became u-u or "w", and the other English letters were discarded.

This form of the language, called Middle English, while still difficult at times, is comprehensible to the modern English reader. Recall Geoffrey Chaucer's Wife of Bath from Canterbury Tales (translated):

Experience, though noon auctoritee
Were in this world, were right ynogh to me
To speke of wo that is in marriage;
For, lordynges, sith I twelf yeer was of age
Thonked be God, that is eterne on lyve,

Difficult to read? Isn`t it? Yes indeed. Don't worry, this station called *history* is about to end. Be glued to develop this habit of going to the origin. While navigating through the station, the journey is taking us through some fantastic learning about the basics that will instill the secrets to quick, fast, and firm learning and competitive edge. And I must tell you; I hate the word "Competition." Let us all replace the word *competition* with *complementariness*. I believe that instead of competing with others, we can act as complements to each other. That is a magical thing I learned. Ok, so going back to the journey let me take you further.

Modern English

With the introduction of the printing press (invented by Johann Gutenberg in 1448) to Great Britain in the mid-15th century by William Caxton, English became more standardized, and modern English appeared. Sometime in the mid-16th century, V and U were split into two letters, with U becoming the vowel, and V, the consonant. In 1604, Robert Cawdrey published the first English dictionary, the Table Alphabeticall, and about this time, J was added to create the modern English alphabet we know today. And the rest, as they say, is history.

We say mistakes make you learn things, but don't believe this and never follow this path of learning. If you take this path, one life would not be enough to make all the mistakes ourselves and learn. You also have a way of learning from other`s mistakes. So, right at the time when you concluded with the Alphabet A as the first step towards learning and here by, A, I Mean Acceptance:

So, by sailing through the *history* station, we discovered an important and the most pivotal step towards learning- how to learn.

HEAL your learning:

1. **H; HISTORY:** The *history* station paves the way for the *future* station. Never let your mind pass through without knowing the history or origin of the stuff you are learning. Without a starting point, how can you think of an ending point? I am right, or am I right?

2. **E; EVOLUTION:** Focus on how it evolved over time and the stages through which something went through; in this case, we saw the evolution of the English alphabets, and don't you think it is fascinating to know it. It paves the foundation stone for interest in the subject matter being considered.

   You have also evolved since you were born, and imagine how magical has been your evolution where you had tiny small hands with fingers close to the thickness of laptop charger wire, and you barely could stand, but now it has been magically nurtured to have grown manifold times.

3. **A; ACCEPTANCE:** Acceptance of the fact that you don't have a clear idea or knowledge about a certain thing. With acceptance, you control & command your mind by refusing to accept opinions offered by your notorious mind. By accepting what you don't know, you

remove the layer that prevents us from real learning.

4. **L; LAYER REMOVAL:** Learning without this is so firm that any external factor fails to shake off the learning. Without this layer, the real learning hooks and sticks to your mind rather permanently that can`t be stunned.

Ok, so after healing your learning as you are plagued by *DIGITAL DEMENTIA*, remember I mentioned this in the very beginning. So, what is digital dementia, hey hey hey!! Hold yourself.

Let us practically *HEAL* our learning first before boarding for the next station straightaway:

If you really want to gain control of your mind that wanders all around and makes *NOISE*, let us start our journey of becoming the CEO of our minds that is not influenced by external factors.
So, in case you find it difficult to control, and your mind repeatedly reminds you to google out this term to find the meaning, gain control & order that you refuse to take orders from the notorious mind and let it take orders from you. And the order you should give here is not to google out this term till I say.

And if you did google it out, thinking "Who is watching me, let me google it," then my friend, you are in deep trouble, and if you didn't google it till now, then you have begun your journey towards becoming the CEO.

Let us not google it till I say, and I bet you will find it difficult not to google out this term.

So, try applying the HEAL principle in learning something. Only after you have applied HEAL for learning something, say a new word: *Quarantine* (I read this word today for the first time in my daily *Golden-hour*), you should board for the upcoming stations, or else the *price* would be higher if you travel without ticket i.e., the HEAL principle.
Yes, HEAL is the ticket to learning.

So, before you tell me that now HEAL has been repeated a good number of times, you all need to show me the tickets please, time to audit, and find the defaulters.

Are you wondering what I am talking about or how can you show me your ticket? Don't worry, apply HEAL to 5 different learnings of your choice. So, to be quick: what can be better than applying HEAL principle in understanding COVID-19. If you have carefully read the chapter on the pandemic, I have tried to apply HEAL.

Additionally, I will suggest you learn five new words right away till I am back after a good strong coffee. That is just my suggestion. You are the heroes, so you have full decision-making power what to learn, and then I am waiting about to finish my coffee, come on, hurry up.

Before knowing the *"What"* of anything, try to know about the *"wherefrom"* and how did it come into being what it is today. It gives you a significant advantage, and that also instills genuine confidence.

You will come across this quote several times in this journey-*"If we can`t do big things, let us do small* *things in big ways."* I am wondering how many of us are awake to celebrate Republic Day as we have midnight culture of wishing happy birthdays. Are we patriotic enough to stay awake for our national festival?

So, I am done with my coffee, it`s 71st Republic day today, and we as INDIA stand as tall as never before, and I am getting Goosebumps with a strong patriotic feeling. And the first thing I did today when I opened my eyes was to listen to the national anthem and a song which is close to my heart, Maa Tujhe Salaam, by A.R Rahman.

This day reminds me of a poem by Rabindranath Tagore that was my daily morning school prayer, which still motivates me in my tough times:

I recommend you to learn it wholeheartedly, and not only learn but try to understand the in-depth meaning. Please don't hurry up reading. Go through this poem several times till you can start feeling goosebumps. It strikingly relates to the current negative situations.

Where the mind is without fear and the head is held high
Where knowledge is free
Where the world has not been broken up into fragments
By narrow domestic walls
Where words come out from the depth of truth
Where tireless striving stretches its arms towards perfection
Where the clear stream of reason has not lost its way
Into the dreary desert sand of dead habit
Where the mind is led forward by thee

Into ever-widening thought and action
Into that heaven of freedom, my Father, let my country awake

As I already told you that the 71st Republic Day celebration is personally extraordinary for me. The reason: My heaven; Vinay Nagar Bengali Senior Secondary School was chosen to perform in front of the world. And this has been one of the best memorable moments of my life.

So, are you ready to board for the next station? Have you HEALED your learning? If not, I would request you to try it at least if not master it. I would encourage all of you to HEAL your learning always, and you will see wonders happening in your life.

The below-mentioned statements should serve as the entry gate for the next journey

"In a conflict between the heart and the brain, follow your heart."
"The powers of the mind are like the rays of the sun when they are concentrated, they illumine."
"The mind is but the subtle part of the body. You must retain great strength in your mind and words."

—Swami Vivekananda

Let us start our next *journey*:

Chapter 4: Inside the mind

- Characters inside the mind.
- Brain- A Closer Look
- Organizational Psychology
- Mind v/s Brain
- Origin of the term, Mind – Applying HEAL

Characters inside the mind.

This chapter will serve as a ticket to the next lesson on learning how to learn. So I urge everyone to pay your closest attention here. Also, look for ***action points*** not just consuming information would help. This is magical and *my first love of life* i.e., *learning*. I have developed deep love with how our mind facilitates the learning process. Over the years, this is one skill that I have developed with the help of *failures* in the beginning, *repeat failures* after starting, *experimentation* in the middle, *and self-realization* in the progress resulting into experiential learning. I fell in love with the process of learning eventually. It has served as an optimization tool which can be applied at almost everything. I still wonder how lucky I have been to discover its magic.

I had my first encounter with my *darling, learning process* at the age of around 12 after being thrown out of my school for the poorest of the poor performance. You will encounter this story later in the book. Cutting the long story short, this incident served as one of the dots in my life that later so well connected with the other dots to help me write a book and enter in the world of knowledge sharing and life-long learning. We will learn tips and techniques of learning in detail in the next chapter. Here, in this lesson, we will build the foundation first and then the tall monument.

Have you ever gone to a water park? How does it feel like? It is so illuminating and energizing to go and get refreshed. And, yes, you have so many rides to rock on and scream.
You won`t believe that I have never been to a water park, but still, when someone from my family and social circle share pictures and about their enjoyment, it gives me heebie-jeebies.

So, let us go together on a delightful ride to one of the waterparks. The biggest water parks in the world.

https://www.travelandleisure.com/trip-ideas/family-vacations/biggest-water-park-in-world
Did you know Tropical Islands Resort is the biggest indoor water park, or Ice Land Water Park, a sprawling series of crystal blue pools in the United Arab Emirates, or Caribbean Bay Water Park in South Korea. These are some of the big ones.

30 miles south of Berlin, inside a former airship hangar, which is frosted in the snow in the winter, is a wonderful vacation destination. Tropical Islands Resort is the biggest indoor water park in the world and

manages to keep its visitors warm (though not dry) all year.

It covers an area of more than 16 acres—that's more than the size of six city blocks—and can host up to 6,000 guests at a time. The water park caters to vacationers of all kinds. For kids, there's a paddling area with toys, as well as a waterslide and a water play table.

There's also Tropino Club, which offers bumper boats, miniature cars, and air hockey. There are also bigger waterslides means that even parents are guaranteed not to get bored.

But wait, isn't the journey here about the mind? Oh yes, hold on the instant gratification monkey that I am sure must have visualized about the park - blue water, high rides, cool breeze, and what not, or maybe you started to go back to the memory lane of your most recent visit to any waterpark?

Let us start the journey to a place that has built all of the world`s humungous & giant structures. So, ever wondered, from where do these come? Before making anything, however big or small, it is first built inside a fantastic machine. Can you guess it?

Oh yes! You guessed it right. Treat yourself with a hot cup of coffee for the answer. I may also give you a treat for this answer if we meet sometime in the future and will be more than happy to provide you with a treat.

So, the answer is MIND. It is such a blissful creation by the almighty that I still wonder how such a thing could be built that has zillion speed, infinite storage, such a strong visual memory. Processing speeds of a millionth of a second. And I can`t stop myself from talking about the MIND. So finally, let us start an enthralling journey to our own mind.

Later in the chapter, we will encounter three different characters that reside in our minds. I must tell you now so that you don't question me how they could board our journey without a ticket. And do you wonder how I met these characters? It is Tim Urban, a Tedx Speaker whom I encountered while watching one of his videos during my *Golden-Hours* (to be discussed in upcoming chapters).

The three characters are:

1. The instant gratification monkey
2. The Panic Monster
3. The rationale self

Sounds good? Or still, wondering who these are? Let us quickly go back to our school or college days to understand. I want you to remember the time when you had to complete your assignments/projects.
So, what we did is we made plans to complete a sixty pages project by writing two or three pages daily so that we could complete in within a month quickly.

Ok, this seems a perfect plan. After fifteen days, we realize we haven't started yet, so make a brand-new plan that has the power potential to complete the project in fifteen days by writing six pages a day now. We feel relaxed, as we have covered for the last fifteen days and also made our plan more efficient.

And, in the last fifteen days, we have done very gratifying acts like watching the most beautiful girl in the college and thinking about how to get the girl`s attention. Some of you may have gone to the extent of asking your female friends to help you out to talk to the girl. And, with your so-called team, you created a script with the scene that when the beauty enters the library and tries to find her semester two books, she was not able to find. Why couldn't she find it?

Because you with your team hid the book, oh yes, finally, this is the moment you created where the beauty is in need and you, the hero, enter in the scene with exactly the book that the beauty was looking. Bang on, the girl is impressed, and you won. You know I had once created this script and it turned out to be effective!!!!!

So here, our best friend is the instant gratification monkey that does the entire tasks basis the present moment and knows how to live life to the fullest. This monkey knows how to be in the moment and takes the responsibility of your gratification and happiness. It is so caring for your happiness that it even sacrifices essential things for you for the sake of your instant gratification. It offers care for your gratification of impressing the girl rather than executing the plan for completing assignments.

So, in doing so, you wake up one day realizing that tomorrow is the last day to submit the assignments, and now you don't have even time to plan.

So, you follow some quick fix. Can we remember what we did in this situation? Yes, of course, you can.

We called our fire-fighter friends to get a copy of any assignment written by a senior.

And the final plan is executed to write in such exciting handwriting that the professors cannot understand most of the things. And lastly, you find yourselves completing the assignment watching your wristwatch ten times in a one-minute wondering that you have five more minutes to submit. And after submission, you realize you forgot to write sure thing like your roll number, and the project name. Phewwwww, so you dare to ask your professor to take it back to write the forgotten things, and you proudly handover the assignment with a big prayer; "Oh God! Please save me."

Wow! What a great battle fought.
The Panic Monster made the final plan (the savior), and the instant gratification only fears this personality, so the moment the monster emerged, the gratification monkey flew away and hid.

Getting back to where we started with the plan and the personalities associated.

1. 2/3 pages per day. Completion days = 30 –
   The rationale mind
2. 6/7 pages per day. Completion days = 15 –
   The rationale mind
3. Impressing the beauty plan
   Instant Gratification Monkey
4. Last-minute completion of project
   The Panic Monster

I am sure you must have these three, and still, they reside in our minds. Most of the time, the monkey proves to be a winner. And, the monster is the only savior which most often is sleeping until something significantly big happens like last day for meeting deadline. The boss had called for performance review. Principal had called you with your guardian to school or college.

What if we relate the panic monster and lockdown in other countries during the pandemic? India has been courageous and smart enough to go for a lockdown instead of satisfying the instant gratification monkey of economic well-being and technological advancement. Unlike other counties, India very early with the help of the rationale self, realized the importance of social distancing and lockdown and implemented it effectively. Though there had been hiccups and challenges of mass exodus, opposition from the political parties. And to add to the pandemic, we all have seen a *fatal event*, in Nizamuddin, which alone offered more than 2000 infections across the country. But given the fact the population and density of our country, we fared much better than the rest of the places unlike Italy, Spain & America etc.

These places are still struggling with lakhs of infected patients with over daily deaths of more than 1000 patients at the time when I was writing this draft.

Without getting into the boring topic of biology and anatomy of the brain, let us straight forward galvanize for a tour of one of the most exciting parts of the brain when it comes to neurogenesis (learn more about this in the next chapter Learning How To learn) and this is the hippocampus. This is important for learning, memory, mood, and emotion. Before diving in it will be worth to understand our brain and its various parts related to learning so that we can make the most of it.

The key is not to have the information but the access to ***action points*** which will help us to decode the secrets of the magical process of learning.

Don't take this as a biology class as it may feel like. Let us take it as an ***action class*** as we will also look at the nitty-gritties of taking care of our mind to optimize it the way we want to update our version.

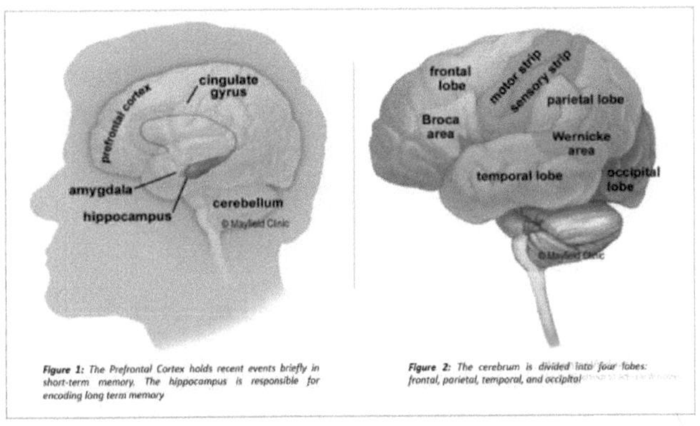

Figure 1: *The Prefrontal Cortex holds recent events briefly in short-term memory. The hippocampus is responsible for encoding long term memory*

Figure 2: *The cerebrum is divided into four lobes: frontal, parietal, temporal, and occipital*

Source: Mayfield Brain & Spine. Its certified info materials are written and developed by the Mayfield clinic.

In figure 1, it is interesting to note what role each part plays and how the brain takes care of our memory. Memory in itself is a complex process that includes three phases: **encoding** (deciding what information is important), **storing** and **recalling**. Different areas of the brain are involved in different types of memory. Your brain has to pay attention and rehearse in order for an event to move from short term memory to long term memory – called **encoding**.

Short term memory:

Also called working memory occurs in the prefrontal cortex. It stores information for about 1 minute and its capacity is limited to 7 items. For e.g. it enables you to dial a phone number someone just told you. It also takes care of reading and plays a pivotal role in enabling to memorize the sentence you have just read so that the next one makes sense.

Long-term memory:

It is processed in the hippocampus of the temporal lobe and is activated when you want to memorize something for a longer time. The memory has unlimited content and duration capacity. It contains personal memories as well as facts and figures.

Skill Memory:

It is processed in the cerebellum, which relays information to the basal ganglia. It stores procedural learned memories like trying a shoe, playing an instrument, or riding a bike.

In the figure 2, we will restrict ourselves to get to know about only **frontal lobe.**

It plays important role in:

- Personality, behavior, emotions
- Judgement, planning, problem-solving
- Speech: Speaking and writing
- Body Movement
- Intelligence, concentration & Self-awareness

***Irresistible* facts on frontal lobe:**

The most interesting part about frontal lobe is that it is not fully developed until the age of 25 or sometimes more. It is the last thing for the brain to get matured.

According to Robert M. Sapolsky who holds degrees from Harvard and Rockefeller Universities and is currently a Professor of Biology and Neurology at Stanford University and a Research Associate with the Institute of Primate Research, National Museums of Kenya. His most recent book is Behave: The Biology of Humans at Our Best and Worst.

The brain`s part are all developed and mature except this frontal cortex. This is what makes an adolescent, adolescent. All the gory behavior or *amazing* behavior of teenagers can be attributed to its nature of not being full developed till a certain age. So you must be wondering, how is this information is going to help us? Why do some teenagers become business tycoons early in their 20`s despite this fact?

To help you with the above question I have some interesting facts to present here. According to Sapolsky, "because your frontal cortex is the last part to develop it's the part of the brain that is most sculpted by environment and experience—and least constrained by genes," That's the greatest news! Your adventure levels, openness, experience, and influences at 25 years old will shape who you are when you're 60.

"The sensation-seeking and the risk-taking; the highs are higher and the lows are lower," he says. Teenagers are more adventurous and more heroic during this time—but can also be more violent and impulsive.

This means somehow, though we don't have any direct means to be in control of how our brain develops but we can play a very pivotal role in the development of our frontal cortex as already said it is most sculpted by environment and experience and least constrained by genes. This further indicates that we can of course choose the type of environment to be in, what kind of experiences do we indulge in, though not every experience will be in your control. But to some extent we can play a huge role in the way we want our brains to be developed.

For the ones, especially ***parents, teachers and seniors***, who blame and target all harsh words for teenagers, we need to understand that it is the absence of fully developed prefrontal cortex responsible for their behavior. As discussed, environment and experience have a great deal to play here, how they will grow and mature depends on your behavior in handling them. Giving them a harsh tone, creating an environment of blaming develops them that way. Giving an environment of listening and acceptance allows them to similarly develop the habit of acceptance and inclusiveness.

We have to allow them the environment and behavior that we expect from them. Bullying them over their little mistakes and making them feel horrible for their failures, exposes them to an environment that shapes their development and they adopt retaliation as a habit which later on grips their mind when they are out as professionals. And I am no exception. I have myself left so many jobs earlier in haste over small petty issues that I wasn't able to deal with. But now I realize how stupid it was to have such a behavior.

Now especially for the ***HR and job professionals.*** An understanding of this phenomenon can certainly help in *employee retention, engagement, controlling attrition rates, employee relations team*.

On the employee`s part, it will be worth it to understand what is expected out of us so that we don't let ourselves land in situations due to our quick impulse and rather act more sensibly.

A tale worth sharing here is to understand organizational Psychology and behavior patterns. From the last decade or so there has been a lot of discussion and surveys about *consumer behavior*. It is time now to discuss *employee behavior* and *organization behavior*. We will also discuss very useful concepts like the concepts generational integration and intelligence.

Generation	Born	Socio-Economic Environment	Career Goals	Mentoring	Retention	Workplace
Gen Z	2005 Onwards	Gig Economy, Technology, Social Security	Gen z prefers communicating through social networks and instant messaging and considers email so yesterday. Is just starting to enter workforce			Office/Home-Desire Flexibility
Gen Y (Millennials)	90`s till About 2005	Growing Economy, low need for money because of parents stability, making money from vocation	Multiple careers, multiple industries	Constant, Continuous feedback	Personal relationships and purpose	
Generation X	70`s till late 80`s	Security for family, vertical growth	Transferable career	Not Required	Exposure and opportunities	
Baby Boomers	50`s to late 60`s	Creating wealth in stable economy, Building, & Cashing in on skills	Build a single career	No negative feedback	Salary/ stability	Office only
Traditionalists	1940`s	Thankful for a career offering stability	Build legacy, one company	Not required	Loyalty	

Five Generations in the Global Workforce

You can gain some interesting insights form the table above. Let us try to connect the behavior to the frontal lobe phenomenon development with age responsible for erratic behavior according to its presence or absence.

From a very famous Arab Proverb, that says *"People resemble their times more than they resemble their parents"*, we may infer that it holds absolutely true in this context.

An understanding of the behavior according to generations to which they belong can help in taking key decisions for organization and forming policies.

I met a psychologist at one of the conferences at NASSCOM, Old Gurgaon center about this topic and she presented a very funny yet true pictorial representation that I must bring here.

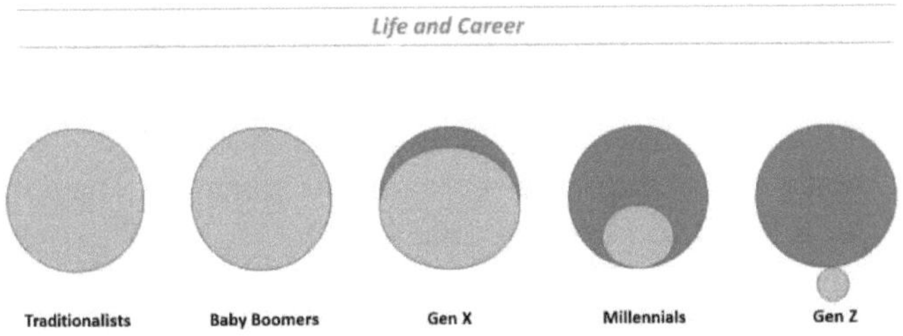

Here, we try to look at how life and career are related differently for different generations. It is worthwhile to note from the above picture that for the *traditionalists & Baby boomers*, the entire life revolved around their career. Anything apart from this may be social gathering or an activity that didn't fall within their circle life aka career would be paid little heed.

This belief changes from the *generation X onwards* where career and life doesn't necessarily mean the same. Most of the life still revolves around career yet life meant other activities as well. These activities may mean a bit of sports, social gathering, and spending time with friends and family.

As you observe for the millennials, life and career are different though a substantial part of career and life coincides. But the feeling of freedom, independence, breaking of rules, chilling out socially gains popularity. And now they consider career as a small part of their life. Where it is just a means to explore and live for your desires.

And the best one is for the Gen Z, where life and career are entirely different. Career and personal life should be kept separate and none should have the influence on the other. Now career is out of life. Life is much more than the career one pursues. They are treated as two separate entities.

Let us identify ourselves with the Psychological career stages. This comes from the ***"Theory of Career Development by Donald Super"***

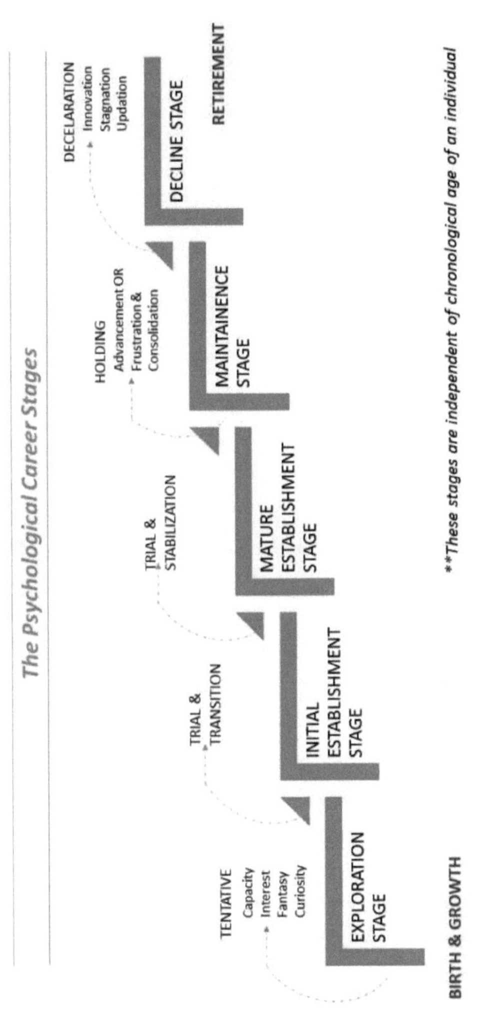

It will be interesting to note that we can identify ourselves within one of these stages. The best part is that the stages are independent of the chronological age of an individual. But still we can relate to our age to some extent. That is the answer to why some early twenties become successful entrepreneurs and the others in 40`s and 50`s struggle with their maturity.

With the understanding of the psychological stages of career, the behavior and aspirations of different generations, we will be in a better position for decision making.

Let us now connect understanding of the frontal lobe and the psychological stages of career one by one

1. **Exploration Stage** (Typically 20 to 30 years of age)**:** Here the career choices are more driven by interest and fantasy. Realistic job images are yet to form. Their focus in on identifying career dreams, trying to narrow career options, experimenting etc. the major drivers at this stage are fantasy image of offices, lack of self-awareness assisted by glorified self-images. It is further supported by lack of self-modulation and general impatience with life. Peer and social pressure are at peak here. That is why, after throwing off a decent job opportunity at this stage we find pleasure and achievement and ask guidance from another friend who has done the same thing. That means all the possibility of ***choosing the wrong guide*** (Learn more about choosing the right guide in the next chapter).

   The common behavior patterns observed are job-hopping, random selection of choices, less than normative time spent on each role, disengagement of performance struggles. We in this stage tend to discard feedback at a large level and we rely on our friends of the same age for feedback and guidance. So actually the feedback just becomes a dishonest praise as friends back their friends instead of giving honest feedback. The thoughts that *I deserve more, and my boss knows nothing, I can work better than him if given a chance* remains dominant.

Wondering why is there a surge in exploration? The answer lies in the development of the frontal cortex.

Nevertheless, it is the absence of fully developed frontal lobe that makes us behave the way least expected. Frontal lobe helps in making choices and taking decisions. On the other side, lack of development of frontal lobe yields

- Risky behavior
- Impulsive decision making
- Confusion when there is a choice
- Intensified response to positive and negative stimuli
- Inability to perceive reality

For us who are at this stage, few questions might help to curb these behaviors

- How well do I know my parents vocation?
- How closely I appreciate my parent`s struggle?
- Are my friends matured enough and the right guide for my career?
- How often do I get into career conversations at home and the nature?
- Is social media grass really greener?

So the next time you find yourselves at such a stage it is better to save yourselves from risky behaviors.
And for the organizations, if you find such a behavior, be at ease in dealing with them, their frontal lobe is under construction!!!

Let us have a look at the exploration cycle. I am sure all of us have gone through these cycles.

After going through multiple such cycles they gain a reality check. They discover that:

- Everything has ***uncool*** side.
- I have strengths and development gaps.
- I will have to struggle.
- I will have to fend for myself.

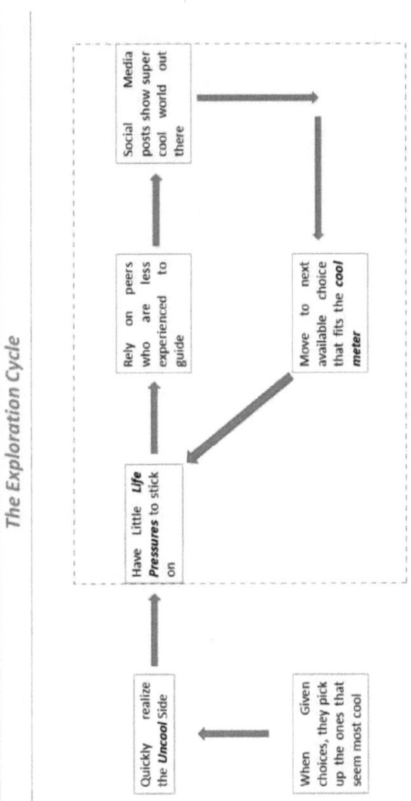

2. **Initial Establishment Stage** (Typically 25 to 35 years of age): Here elimination sets in. We can relate so some phrases like:
    - I know what I don't want to do
    - I know what I will not enjoy
    - I know what I am not good at

At this stage, one is willing to test personal boundaries. It is marked by intense desire to move away from confusion. The drivers that serve at this stage are intense search for passion, can differentiate real from unreal, acceptance of flaws in reality. Also some behavioral traits are observed. People at this stage set up personal challenges to succeed. They also say yes to difficult aspects of jobs for longer time. They tend to stick with activities and jobs for longer time while having willingness to listen to feedback and direction. These are the early positive signs of maturity.

3. **Mature Establishment stage** (Typically 35 to 45 years of age): With all the exploration and impulsive decisions taking a backseat here, the transition period is well served by the stage discussed above. That is what we call the learning curve. During this period, it is hoped that a suitable occupation is found and the person engages in those activities that help him or her earn a permanent place in it. The focus relies on:
    - Trying to determine the value of career choice
    - Gaining work experience related to own career choice
    - Beginning to stabilize within the career
    - Continuing to increase self-understanding

Here the drivers shift a lot in comparison to the earlier stages. Here one develops his or her understanding of the world of work-post experimentation. More goal oriented behavior is seen with desire for success, growth and making a mark. This period is also marked by the life roles change as people here are usually young family with liabilities and responsibilities. People here also desire a bit of flexibility and independence to the needs of the family. Co-worker comfort is also developed here. And the most important, age provides authority.

The behavior traits generally seen is desire to meet/exceed targets and prove your own worth. These people are also the ones who will invest additional hours at work.

For rest of the two stages, i.e., ***Maintenance and the Decline stage*** I am sure you can well imagine the behavior as well as the drivers. Here one key concept is that few of them in these stages can go back to the exploration and initial establishment stage by learning the *art of re-invention* (you Read about this in the chapter, *The Quarantine Era*). Moreover, the people who re-invent themselves at this stage have the advantage of developed frontal cortex which helps them to be more pragmatic this time.

Mind & Exercise:

What if you came to know that you can do something that can have immediate and long lasting results on your brain? The best news is that you can experience the effects almost instantly. It can help in being better than normal and average person. It can also help in dealing with stress levels and more complex problems of depression beside significant others.

I have been fascinated by the process of learning as I designate it as the first love of my life. Over the last couple of years, say around 5 or 6 years this field has drawn much of my attention. With every step, I became more interested in getting to know how can we deliberately shape up our brains and can optimize it to produce extraordinary results. As I developed keen interest in its functioning as it is the most complex and powerful structure known to mankind I realized that the world we see around us and to get narrower whatever you see around the place where you are sitting right now is a manifestation of human brain.

Imagine how such a small part of our body has enormous potential to change and shape the world around us. The key lies in understanding how our own brain functions. The next important thing to know is what kind of environment suits our brain. Each and every brain is unique in the way it functions and operates. You must know and study what and how you learn the best. There is "no one size fits all" technique here. You have to practice and become aware what your brain requires.

Despite the fact that our brains function differently, yet there are few things that can be done as a universal practice that will produce astounding results. After spending my entire career in learning from development field, figuring out the best training practices, the best ones that work and the worst that doesn't, I have developed a deep interest to look and share with you the code of learning.

As discussed in upcoming chapters about my first interaction with the learning process way back in 2004 when I was thrown out of the school for poor grades, I did uncountable experiments to decode the secrets of learning. The best *subject* of the experiment was *myself*. So, I had nothing to lose, neither my reputation nor the mishaps from the experiments.

Soon after a year, when my experiments with the learning process produced some astonishing results by topping the charts in the entire school, I was sure that this is going to shape my career. Bang on!! I had discovered my first love of life in my early teens. I had little idea that there is a huge career in this domain which later on became my full time profession.

Accidently, I had done a wonderful thing then. When I was thrown out, I didn't think ***about what to learn,*** rather I thought much about ***how to learn.*** It paved the way that that has come this far. I can still relate to that era of omnipresent failures in every field, except in one, i.e., physical activity. You call it exercise, activity, sports or whatever. But it has some amazing effect on our brain. I was not mature enough to understand it then, but now going through various experiments on myself, numerous research papers and journals, listening to endless neuroscientists, and TEDx speakers over a period of more than close to two decades, I realized that this is worth knowing and sharing with the world. I want all of you to reap benefits of understanding the functioning of your ***personalized*** unique brains.

You don't need to put such tedious efforts as I did, instead you can benefit from my unique experience that can serve as the starting point for your own journey. It is still such a pity that most of the educational institutions & Corporates boast about

what to learn, I have rarely seen them focusing on ***how to learn***.
This shift of focus can entirely change the learning industry.

All my childhood have been of high activity levels be it sports like cricket, badminton or anything that made me sweat, or running early in the morning or taking short walks in between study sessions, or reading aloud while walking on a terrace. With all these little experiments and more, I connected the dots, after growing up as you can well imagine that my frontal lobe was still under development.

Cutting long story short, I have come to the conclusion that it is worth sharing and applying. I realized that most of the things that I did unknowingly as exercise or physical activity actually had shaped my performance which is a growing and expanding field of study i.e., neuroscience. After going through what the literature and other experiments in this field had to offer me to study, the results that I found was exciting enough. It had essentially everything about the benefits of exercise on our brain`s functions. Better attention and focus, memory (both long term and short term), mood and curiosity to learn more and what not.

Let me ask a question here. How many of you remember your first kiss? Or your life`s first ever crush? May be a personal question but we will restrict ourselves for the purpose of study and understanding our brain here. (And let me remind you that this is a self-help book and not a romantic novel!! Hey hey! So come back!!) Imagine how a moment that didn't last for long but had altered the way we behaved with that person before and after the kiss. Such a short moment but had a long lasting impression on our mind. Remember the first time you failed in a subject or the first time you boarded a flight. Such things form an everlasting memory.

Wendy Suzuki, an expert from neuroscience, also explains in one of her finest TED talks that "Exercise is the most transformative thing that you can do for your brain today for the following three reasons:"

1. It has immediate effects on your brain. A single workout that you do increases the levels of neurotransmitters like dopamine, serotonin, and noradrenaline. These chemicals increase the good mood that is exactly what was happening to me when I had earliest encounter of learning.
2. It helps in Attention Management which will last for a significant number of hours.
3. It helps in improving on reaction time which aids in decision making like pressing on the brake pads when driving a car as soon as realizing of impending mis-happening on road or catching a ball that is aimed at your face.

She further explains that, "exercise changes brains anatomy, physiology and functions."

The common findings in neuroscience that are worth sharing here are:

1. Exercise helps in neurogenesis i.e., the development of new brain cells (see more on this topic in the upcoming chapter).
2. Improved attention function dependent on the prefrontal cortex. You increase your focus with exercise and not only that, it also increases the volume of the hippocampus.

3. It has most important aspects of protective effects on your brain.

I am sure you must be wondering, "Ok, so how much minimum exercise we should do to get all these in place? Isn't it?"

I will tell you the most interesting fact about exercise as also explained by Wendy, that exercise is **free**. Yes you heard it right it is absolutely **free.** May be that is the reason why talking about exercise is one thing and actually doing it is something different. And my dear *delegation* or *outsourcing* principle doesn't apply here. So you have to do it yourselves. But you don't necessarily have to take a gym membership for that matter or otherwise a club membership.

You don't even have to set a target of losing 5 kg a month or have 16" biceps. If you dream to enter in to the modelling world then maybe it will seem to be justified.

The optimum exercise for upkeep of your $\mathbf{B^2}$ i.e. the Brain and the Body is anywhere between 3-5 days a week for at least 30 minutes. The next question, what kind of exercises do you prefer? The answer is very simple in developing small habits of choosing staircase instead of lift and escalators, power walk, getting off the bus one stop before your destination and whatever is possible in daily routines to accommodate.

I recommend the below exercises. These have proven far-reaching impacts on both the ***brain and the beauty***, I mean the body!!

1. You can look for aerobic exercise that essentially increases your heart rate. Can be as simple as running, skipping, power walks etc.

2. Calisthenics, my personal favorite, where body weight is used for exercise. It is a form of exercise that comprises of movements running, standing, grasping, pushing etc. that exercise large muscle groups (gross motor movements). These exercises with least or no equipment at all and are often performed rhythmically and, as bodyweight exercises.

3. The most important exercise that is least talked about in the fast paced world is ***sleep management.*** It is as important as exercise. Think about it! Are you able to manage your sleep nicely? If not I will recommend to inculcate a habit of *the Golden hour,* through a book named *"The Miracle Morning, by Hal Elrod."* If you are not able to do this exercise, even if you are doing the earlier two, it is of no avail.

A very interesting fact at the time when I was writing this draft: I was unemployed. Yes. I had resigned from my job to join a new company. But soon I was stuck as I had resigned from the previous organization and couldn't join the new one due to lockdown being extended and after lockdown 1 it was time for 2nd and 3rd also.

With the responsibility of entire family, I was no exception to face the brutal effects of Covid-19 and lockdown in particular. And it gets worse when things are uncertain. It was this exercise regime that helped me to maintain my routine and also to be positive. The question was of survival. ***It helped me to focus on what I can do rather than focusing on what I can`t.*** With savings nearing exhaustion with no source of income, it was interesting to embrace the uncertainty. That reminds me of Darwin`s theory of survival of the fittest.

My secret of learning:

I wondered how I could learn things easily at least after realizing that I too can learn. It was not the case till 2005 that I had gained confidence towards learning. I want to share with you the secret of my learning that makes it faster, smarter and enjoyable.

Have you ever thought about teaching? I mean not literally to be teacher professionally. Have you taught anything to someone? May be bicycle, may be how to bowl or how to bat or may be how to make a tie. I strongly believe that humans are inborn teachers.

So the secret lies here. ***Learn with the intention to teach***. Seems so simplistic, isn`t it? What is so big deal about this? Right? Let me answer this for you. It is not as simple as it sounds. It has to do with neuroplasticity (you will learn more on this later in the book). Teaching anything that you learnt facilitates creating of patterns in our brain that drastically adds to the process of learning. This has been my biggest secret and strength though I realized it later. We have certain benefits with learning with this intention.

Firstly, you bring yourselves to a ***state of attention*** (Learn more on this in the upcoming chapter) when you learn with this intention. And the reason is silly yet obvious; no one would want to look like a fool in front of his or her student. So you tend to study with utmost care and getting a step ahead to learn even the slightest of details.

Secondly, it takes care of the ***practice*** that you need for your learning. Practice sometimes gets boring unless you enjoy it. So teaching someone the things you have learnt, plays a great part here.
In one of the book by *Cal Newport*, he has mentioned about *deliberate practice* that sets you apart.
It is different than normal practice. If you practice what you have already mastered, you enjoy it. But when you are learning something new and practice it- the uncomfortable sensation in your head can be best approximated as a physical strain as your new neurons are physically reforming into new configurations. This stretching feels much different than applying a technique you have already mastered.

So, if you are comfortable in your pursuit of being better at something, then you are probably stuck at an *"acceptable level"*. To move beyond acceptable level to a mastery level you must be uncomfortable practicing that makes you stretch. This is how deliberate practice is what matters. Let us move one step ahead beyond practice.

Thirdly, it may be difficult to **give and receive feedback** for ourselves. But when you apply the intention to teach, your mind automatically gives you feedback about the quality of learning. You may lie to your student or a teacher, but you can never lie to yourselves.

Fourthly, you get a ***repeated chance of learning*** while teaching and it helps in learning optimization by updating the current learning version just like any other application on your phone that needs to be regularly updated.

And the benefits are endless. Just try it. *Jim Kwik*, also a pioneer in training tips and techniques enabling us to learn faster, advises this method.

Getting deeper in our minds by applying the HEAL process

http://journalpsyche.org/understanding-the-human-mind/#more-169
For those of you like me who are further interested in exploring the topic, let us now try getting inside the mind by applying the HEAL process learned in the previous chapter through *Freud's Model of the Human Mind.*

Learning from the theory of Sigmund Freud can help us understand different layers of mind very easily. Even though there have been enormous advancements, his basic thoughts are worth to understand and holds a firm ground.

He divides mind into three layers:

1. Conscious
2. Subconscious
3. Unconscious.

Working together, they create our reality. The understanding of the mind has been more dependent on the context of its usage. Let us try to understand few contexts here.

1. Philosophy: The mind may well mean one's personality, identity, and their memories.
2. Religious: The mind houses the spirit, an awareness of God.
3. Science: The mind is the generator of ideas and thoughts.

The broad view of mind to include all mental faculties, feelings, thoughts, volition, and memory gradually developed by around 15th century. Late 19th and early 20th century saw psychology becoming a respected science. The standard focus shifted to the human mind and its role in the behavioral sciences. Today, the concept of the mind and its functions is almost always discussed from a scientific point of view.

The conscious mind serves as a scanner for us. It recognizes an event, prompts a need to react, and then depending on the prominence of the event, store it either in the unconscious or the subconscious area of the human mind where it remains available to us.

Your subconscious is the store house for any recent memories needed for quick recall, such as what your telephone number is or the name of a person you just met. It also holds current information that you use every day, such as your current recurring thoughts, behavior patterns, habits and feelings.

The workhouse of the mind/body experience Freud's subconscious mind serves as the mind`s random access memory (RAM). "Thus the unconscious mind can be seen as the source of dreams and automatic thoughts (those that appear without any apparent cause), the repository of forgotten memories (that may still be accessible to consciousness later), and the locus of implicit knowledge (the things that we have learned so well that we do them without thinking)."

The unconscious mind is where all of our memories and past experiences reside. These are those memories that have been repressed through trauma and those that have simply been consciously forgotten and no longer are important to us (automatic thoughts). It's from these memories and experiences that our beliefs, habits, and behaviors are formed.

https://ipi.org.in/texts/others/mbsharan.php

Let us take an example now. Imagine that we are driving along the highway while returning home. As soon as we reach the neighborhood, we suddenly realize that for the past several minutes, our mind has been somewhere else. We realize that we have been imagining, thinking about things, our mind has been on anything but paying attention to the road. Can we think how we managed to follow traffic signals, watch out for cars, and make the correct turns when we were mentally "not there." Thus, we can infer that there are several things we do without paying proper attention to all at a time, and the pendulum of awareness swings between the "minds" without any difficulty.

This has given rise to a new debate between the "minds", and many of the thinkers and researchers suggest maintaining a balance between the unconscious mind and the conscious/ subconscious mind. They are just a way of describing events - 'conscious' as whatever we are aware of at the moment, and 'unconscious' as everything else – that are useful in the context of therapeutic change

(Bandler & Grinder, 1979). Otherwise, as a whole, we have only one mind.

Now, the question is: By which name should this one mind be known? Those who are working in the field of information processing say that conscious awareness is just the tip of the iceberg. It merely enables us to exert voluntary control and to communicate our mental states to others (Kihlstrom, 1987). Beneath the surface, subconscious information processing co-occurs on many parallel tracks. When we look at a flying bird, we are consciously aware of the result of our cognitive processing but not of our sub-processing of the bird's color, form, movement, distance, and identity. Therefore, from the functional viewpoint, it is the subconscious mind (including unconscious) that takes care of all the processes that are occurring out of conscious awareness. This one mind thus should be known as the subconscious mind.

Conclusion

Now, the question is: What should we conclude from all these? We should not get caught by the words 'conscious', 'subconscious' and 'unconscious'. They are just to describe different functions of the same mind. There are conscious and considered thought, subconscious having recallable memories, habits, and old feelings, and unconscious having forgotten instincts, conditioning and collective or universal experiences. Each of these is accessible to us in some way because they communicate with each other in their own way. We should, therefore, try to develop such a mind which can perceive and judge things rightly making use of all the information – conscious, subconscious or unconscious. According to Vedanta, "The richest soil, the soil of the human mind, lies fallow. If it could be tilled well it would yield golden crops, but since it lies fallow, it yields brambles and thorny bushes and weeds" (Ellis, 1994).

That means, if there are wrong tendencies lying within, they have to be weakened by constant effort.

What is intuition?
The term "intuition" means exactly what it sounds like – in – tuition – an inner tutor or teaching and learning mechanism that takes us forward daily. The dictionary defines intuition as "the perception of truths, facts, etc. without reasoning; the immediate knowledge or learning of something without the conscious use of reasoning; instantaneous apprehension." That means it is a process which perceives things without relying on the senses and gives us a kind of creative awareness by interpreting all the information in a holistic way.

According to Reed and English (2000), by paying attention to the thoughts, feelings, and images that come to our mind, we are learning to tune into our intuition which is a natural gift born in everyone. But it becomes most effective in a person who learns to develop The Intuitive Heart by caring and loving his/her own inner self and of others. In order to have the intuitive experience through The Intuitive Heart, Reed and English suggest the following six steps:

1. **Learn from your breath to trust your intuitive inspiration:** Focus on your breathing and discover how you can trust it to flow naturally, spontaneously, with no effort or control on your part. Intuitive inspiration will come to you automatically.

2. **Make the heart connection:** Let gratitude fill your heart, allowing you to release all concerns. Your heart energy naturally begins to expand. Focus it on the target of your search for intuition.

3. **Invite a memory:** Ask for one of your millions of personal memories to pop into your mind. Without intentionally choosing it, but accepting the first one that comes, trust that within your heart is stored the perfect memory that is just right for this occasion.

4. **Tell your story:** Explore the experience that surrounds that memory. Let your memory be the seed of a story – here's what was going on, here's what happened, here's how it turned out.

5. **Search your heart for wisdom:** See what lessons your story holds. What truths does it contain? What did you learn from that experience? What does this story teach you today?

6. **Learn from feedback:** Note how the teaching story relates to the focus of your quest for intuition. How can you use this new perspective to respond to your current situation differently?

"The Illiterate of the 21st century will not be those who cannot read and write, but those who can`t learn, unlearn and relearn."

— Alvin Toffler

Chapter 5: Learning how to learn (Inside out Approach)

- Optimizing your brain
- Specially crafted for students, professionals and parents.
- The 7 Wonders of learning or The 7 Principles of learning.

- Action is knowledge
- Principle 2: Finding the right Guide
- Principle 3: Don't expect anything for free, not even learning. It is against the law of nature.
- Principle 4: HEAL Principle
- Principle 1: State of Mind
- Principle 5: Autosuggestion- Do you like questions
- Principle 6: The Zorro Circle
- Principle 7: Tetris Effect

I am infinitely fascinated by the wonderful process of learning. And I call it the 1st wonder of the world that has existed from the very start of civilization. It was the process of learning through which we learnt to walk, talk and also to stalk. Hey hey!! Don't take me too seriously. And that is the case with learning. It isn't a thing to be taken seriously. It is to be enjoyed thoroughly and the process is miraculously satisfying and pleasant only if you learn the art of enjoying it.

This journey is perhaps the best and my most favorite. How many mobile numbers do you remember these days? Pause and think for a minute. Let me guess. Most probably you remember yours and some of you, if you have recently changed your numbers; you must have saved your own number on your phone. Some of you may remember your parents' mobile number. Ok, who else's. Some of your close friends' numbers. Umm!! May or may not.

Let us move now. How many of you will have to use a calculator to get to the answer of 75^2? And, if that was easy for you, what about 105^2. If you find difficulty in doing these *small* pieces of stuff and want to know the solutions fasten your seatbelts tightly and be glued to what is going to come now.

I wonder, and I am pretty sure that you all will agree with me that we all were taught what to learn and not how to learn. Gathering and amassing as much information as possible has been the primary goal for students, teachers, and professionals. But there is a problem with this statement as information is not knowledge. Very often, information is confused with education & learning. The yardstick of academic & professional competency is sadly the amount of information one has. And I am not against the fact that we should have information and should be well informed.

But my dear friends, ***information*** is not knowledge, but the ***action*** is. What is the use of information which you can`t apply? This doesn't mean you have to apply all the chemical reactions that you studied and all the facts. This would be a disaster, and you will not head anywhere.

Before proceeding, I must tell you that you have to pay close attention to every single word here that you are about to read. Let`s go and rock.

You may also have heard this very common phrase about book reading, "book reading is useless", "why do people waste time in reading books", "book readers are boring" etc.

Yes, they are right and you heard it right. Why am I calling them right is because all these statements are limited to book reading. *Book reading actually doesn't help unless you apply the things you learnt.People who read books actually waste time by just reading and not applying the learnings from the books.And yes, book readers are boring when they don't apply it in their real lives.* And I really feel pity for those who read book as a sedative at bedtime. They are not aware what are they missing.

I learned the art of learning when I was thrown out of my school for poor performance. I will not share the entire story, but I will surely share how it affected my life and gave me a rebirth. Let me again ask a question here. Apologies, but I have this habit of putting items, and you can`t help it as I am the pilot for this journey.

Who can teach you how to drive a car? I am sure a person who has driven a car and knows how to drive it. But every other person knows how a car is driven, and if you ask anyone, you will get the guidance about steering, accelerator, clutch, brake, and gear. But just knowing how a car is driven, is that enough? A person who himself has not driven a car tells you how to drive. How absurd is this? So, whose mistake is this? Of course, not the person who gave you tips on driving, but it is you who choose the wrong guide.

Always believe and choose your guide wisely. And make sure you know that he/she has already done the work that he/she is teaching you. This reminds me of an exciting story of one of my female bosses, who gave me lectures on prioritization of work and building good relationships. And I blindly followed her thinking that she is at such a great position in the company and all the staff members respected her.
Later on, after following her lectures, I found myself struggling with my work being piled up and clashing with my family and a silent girlfriend. I tried hard to solve my problems but wasn't able to.

Later on, I came to know the fact that my boss herself had complex relationships and had always not been able to complete her tasks. So, imagine such a person giving lectures on the things which she was struggling with. I laughed at myself and was so upset with myself for choosing a wrong guide.

Also, one from the big shots. It is about Sir Issac Newton, one of the brightest minds ever on earth, and Benjamin Graham, the author of the bible of Finance & Investment - *"The intelligent investor."*
Newton once invested in stocks in the South Sea company. This was a time when the shares of this company were in high demand in the UK. Once he felt that there was a panic in the market, and he sold all his stock holdings. He made a profit of $7000. It was a 100% profit. After some time, in the influence of others, he again invested in the same company, and this time a significantly higher amount than before. But then, he had to bear a loss of $20000. Later on, he

said that he is an expert at calculating information related to stars but can`t understand the emotions of people, and he asked his friend not to discuss South Sea Company again.

What do we learn here? Wasn`t he a genius? He was indeed a genius in the field of science but not in investing. As he had the least control and understanding of human emotions, he gave in the emotional suggestion and was influenced by others.

But you all are lucky travelers of life, that now as you know, to choose your guide wisely. So, you have all the right to ask a question, am I the right person to tell you about how to learn. I can only do so when I have already learned how to learn.

So, the answer is yes. And trust the driver here and yourself that you have chosen the right guide, at least for this topic.

So, the first principle discussed here has been mentioned. I would love it if you could put some efforts into finding out in previous lines. Let me elaborate on it for you. Meanwhile, you try to find the principle. Going back to the time when I was thrown out of the school back in 2004 partly for poor performance and inability of my father to pay school fees for more than a year. I am tempted to share this story with you to make you understand the journey that accidentally leveraged me to the experiential learning that revealed this principle. This, later on, I found in various books on self-development.

Let us dive back to the day- March 25, 2004.

The set up:

I was sitting in the exam hall (March 25, 2003), experiencing nuclear bombings, I mean my Sanskrit exam and invigilator none other than the Don of my school –Mausmi Madam.
Suddenly, Sanskrit teacher enters and tells me, "Rahul, come on, get off from your place, take your belongings with you, your dad is here to pick you up."
As I heard this, my joy knew no bounds, I felt highly blessed by the almighty to be saved from a dangerous experience of giving Sanskrit exam. As I went outside the classroom full of joy and thinking of enjoying the whole day with cricket and my guitar, dynamite was ready to attack me outside.

The Principal: Do you know how disgusting and irresponsible your son is. You send all your idiots to my school to waste our time and effort. It is because of you people that our school loses its reputation. And moreover, you (my dad) have not paid your dues for over a year, and you expect us to teach your child? Get your son out of here now.

Dad: Speechless (only tears had a word to say).
For the first time in my life, I didn't have an answer to a situation despite being a decent speaker.

I was bewildered at the situation and was in confusion to cry or laugh in this situation.
And as this thought had besieged my mind, I reached home with my dad on the second-hand scooter, which my mom had gifted my father. I was still not able to grasp the situation. Two-three days later, my friends came home and asked, "Come on! What happened,

Rahul? Won`t you play cricket even today? You have not played for three days."

Actually, they couldn't digest the fact that I missed playing cricket. I mean the boy who can forget to take his breath for a day, forget to wear his undergarments, forget to eat but can never ever think of missing cricket for a single day and to be a precise single act of playing cricket right from establishing the stumps in the ground to clearing the pitch.

This fact was indigestible by my friends, and after they asked me some questions, I just told them to please leave me alone. And that was the end of my cricketing career (who aspired to be a great cricketer like Sachin and Glenn Mc Grath.)

Then several serial blasts were waiting for their terror, I mean the process of getting admission in some other school.

Oh God! If somebody would challenge me to hit the fastest century, I could have promised to achieve this feat but giving exam and that too in another school with unknown people seemed horrible and life-threatening to me.

Anyways, I was helpless, so I sat for the exam and those two hours of the exam, My God!!!! It was like sinking in an ocean with no help, struggling for a tiny single breath, with blood circulation matching that of an F-1 Racing record top speed.

Finally, the race ended, and I wished for some magical transformation in my answer sheet, but my wish was soon finished with the entry of the examiner in the principal`s chamber.

Mrs. Princy (The DON of My School, Principal): Can you guess how many marks have you obtained?
I answered 0 or 1(to myself of course! Because this was my capability, not even a single mark greater)
Mrs. Princy: Let me answer this question, my son. It`s 1.

(A I heard this and was about to scream that yuhoooooooo. I guessed it right, my eyes went into my parents` eyes filled with tears, and I was sssshhhhhhhhhhhh.....speechless again.)

Princy: Son, do you deserve to be admitted to our school? Tell me! I think Mr. And Mrs. Thakur (Dad & Mom) your child would not be given admission in any school. Take your son along with you and teach him on your own.

As my parents were about to utter something with a heavy heart, I brought my eyes that were into my parent`s tears right into my madam`s eyes and said- if I am given the admission I will top the class within a year otherwise throw me out of the school whenever you wish. And then the scene was unimaginable. Everybody looked at me as if they were going to eat me.

I still don't know how come I got that much strength and said it with such a great conviction. Maybe due to cricketing challenges, because whenever somebody challenged me, I wouldn't rest for a single moment unless I proved them wrong.

Princy: Are you sure? You know your marks, and still?

I said I am damn sure. I have nothing else to say, and I don't know why the princy admitted me despite my poor marks. But she had seen something that day in me that I understand now when I recollect all those moments. Now I can very well understand why people say "Behind every successful man there is a woman" whether she does or doesn't have 36-24-36 figure or is single or committed! (Just kidding !)

Now I promised because of my nasty taste of loving challenges but didn't know how to achieve this.
In my early days, whenever I tried to study, it seemed like batting with a cricket bat being bowled at by a football, I mean the combination was like that of a 17-year-old beauty with an 80-year-old wrinkled model.
But whenever I felt giving up, I just remembered one saying, "you can`t be defeated unless you accept your defeat" and remembered my parents` tears, which gave me the strength to fight back again. I tried, tried, and tried but unsuccessful in grasping the concepts.

Then one day, I was walking down the roadside (a habit from which I made plans for all my essential matches and field placing) I asked myself ***what do the toppers do and what is the difference between me and that breed of toppers.*** I thought if I could get the answer to this question, I too could be the topper. I looked for the answer for quite several days and realized that there is actually no difference and when there is no difference, why can`t I top the class. I accidentally applied the first principle of learning by asking the above question. I found the solution in the form of a dear friend then, still my closest, named Suraj, who is now an Engineer & working in the UK in a top tech company. He guided me, and gradually, I picked up.

Then I began my real match with studies. It bowled me bouncers, Yorkers, googlies, low full tosses, I was clearly bowled out for few days but soon started out to take singles and after some time even started to hit boundaries I mean begun to grasp the concepts like L.C.M, different mathematical formulae, etc.
Sometimes was run out in between the wicket I mean got stuck in the middle of mathematical problems but soon improved my running between the wickets by grasping the concepts more clearly. Then I started some good field placements by learning the answers thoroughly. And, began to win league matches I mean the unit test and weekly class tests.

I appeared for the first exam of std.VII and stood 6th in the class. Next match 3rd, then 2nd, and my dear then, finale I mean the annual exam topped the class with around about 91 % marks. This was something magical. I was clueless as to how I was able to score so well and that too honestly. I was called by the DON.

Princy: You remember the day Rahul when you had come for admission? I admitted you despite your poor marks. Don`t you want to know why?

I said of course Madam
Princy: Rahul, what impressed me that day was your self-belief and the conviction with which you promised me to top the class. Marks have never been a concern for me. The matter of concern is the real aim of education, which necessarily doesn't mean obtaining

an A-grade in all the exams and completing projects and assignments on time?

I felt glad but was very immature at that time (still I am) to understand what she was trying to say. But now I can understand a bit and from that very bit want to refer back to the principle that is the second one towards learning.

Principle 2: Finding the right Guide

Find a person who has already done & is successfully doing what you want to do.

If you want to be an excellent public speaker, try to connect to an excellent public speaker of any age and see the magic happening, if you want to learn MS-Excel, try finding an excel expert. If you want to learn cooking, don't find an expert. Just purchase a beautiful saree & take your Mom for lunch. The expense will serve as your tuition fee towards learning. Let your mom know about your desire to learn the art of cooking, and she will be more than happy to help you.

In the aforesaid lines, I have also revealed the 3rd principle in learning. Why you had to take your mom out for lunch? Could you guess it? Think for a minute. Apply *STOPP to* find an answer

S: Stop
T: Think
O: Observe
P: Pause
P: Process

So, did you get the answer for the 3rd principle? Ok, if you want me to reveal, let me do it.

Principle3: Don't expect anything for free, not even learning. It is against the law of nature.

You will always need to pay the price in terms of your time, honesty, loyalty, true friendships, and money in many cases. Don't hesitate to pay to learn as learning is priceless, and if you can get that learning by paying a small price, you should. So, follow the law of nature of giving and take. Think of what you can offer to the other person when you think about learning from someone. As Dave Linger has ideally put up, *"You can`t succeed coming to a potluck with only a fork."*

Principle 4: HEAL your learning.

I would urge you all to go back to the starting journey when we began, we did discuss the about *HEALing* our learning or the HEAL process. Moreover, we have also tried to apply it navigating through our journey to take supreme advantage of our learning process.

It is phenomenal that you have come so far. Now I assure you that it is going to be much more enjoyable. Do you think where the principle number 1 is? Did I miss it? Did I intentionally do it? Are you among the ones who forgot to notice that I started from principle number 2 instead of one?

I am sure you will be able to find yourselves close to any of the above questions. Let us now dive deep into the **1st Principle of learning.** It has to be understood in one go, so I would urge all of you to get through this 1st principle at once. Perhaps this is the focal point and epicenter of our journey.

So what was it that brought such a drastic change in me, and before I start, I would urge all of you not to pay attention to what happened to me but the substance that you can get from the incident and the underlying principle because my story is a *story already written*. It is now your turn to write yours by learning magically & using the mentioned principles.

Going back to the time when I was thrown out of the school and initial months that I had to struggle to get enrolled in a decent school. I would like to refer to what happened to the brain (I am now detaching myself from the situation to better explain what happened).

Before Rahul was thrown out of the school, he was in his own comfort zone, and academics would matter for him just as a bright neon color would matter for a blind. He was that aloof from studies. The incidents happened only at the right time to enable him to ignite the thinking process. It actually changed the ***state of his mind.***

Do you go back to a memory lane when you hear a particular song? Are you reminded of your first crush/girlfriend when you watch a movie or a video? Even a fragrance activates our brain and leads us to somewhere. And, I would request all to control themselves here, as fragrance necessarily doesn't associate with romance and more. Don't go to the ideal date that you once planned, followed by something romantic & naughty. Hey hey! So, the point illustrated here is that our memory is associated with emotion and whatever, and whenever we experience and learn with emotion, it can never be forgotten. Neither the girlfriend(s) nor the boyfriend(s), neither a dish nor a flower, neither a line nor a story, neither a book nor a video, and so on and so forth.

The very ***first reason*** for the magical transformation in academics was particularly the ***change in the emotional state of the mind*** of a 12-year-old boy by observing and feeling the pain in his parent`s eyes. Secondly, this very incident planted a seed of ***curiosity.*** The boy now wanted to know ***how it works***. He wanted to decode the secret behind spectacular performance in academics.

Let us decode the first principle by carefully examining the changes in the state of mind of a young boy. And I have good news for all of you. It is possible to change the state the mind the way you want.

The 7 states of mind

1. The state of **R**esponsibility
2. The State of **A**ttention
3. The state of **N**eurogenesis
4. The state of **N**europlasticity
5. The State of **A**ssumed learning
6. The State of **C**uriosity
7. The state of **H**aving a WHY/Purpose

Let us navigate our journey further, and if you have come this far, I assure you that you are going to enjoy learning from now onwards more than ever.

For ease of memory, I am giving you an acronym ***RANNACH.***

This is an Irish word origin, where RANNA means departments, and ACH is an adjectival suffix.

So, let us consider these as the 7 departments of the mental faculties that help you to study through the 1st wonder of the world, a ***University called `Mind`***.

These ***7 states of mind*** have proved to be magical in helping us to learn things quickly and efficiently with an ever-lasting impression engraving rock-solid patterns in our brain. Let me take you all for a deep dive into the above stated spectacular thing one by one to get a grasp. This is all a result of experiential learning of my life till now.

After noticing the eyes of his parents, Rahul saw the tears rolling and dreams being crushed. For the first time, he met super-duper stuff called the REALITY, unlike his superficial world of playing cricket and becoming a star. His state of mind electrified from over-independent thinking to ***the state of responsibility***, which serves as the very first state of mind to be able to learn. Most of the time, we are busy blaming the outer world, our mentors for not teaching us right, our parents for not providing us enough recreational budgets, our bosses for not favoring our ideas, and the list is endless. But seldom have we become responsible for our present condition. The moment we take responsibility on our own shoulders, half the battle is won.

It is only we who are responsible for the present condition. We hear a lot of time employees complaining that their current company is very low-paying, and there is a dearth of opportunities in the market. If it was the case, there wouldn't have been a single employee earning a six-figure salary in the same company that was referred to as a low paying one. And if there was really a dearth of opportunity, a 10th class student named Bhooshita (later discussed in the book) would not have been a chess champion and wouldn't have started Samvedna wherein she teaches the nuances of playing smart chess. There wouldn't be examples of a widow, Nitika Kaul, who lost her husband, Major Vibhuti Shankar Dhoundiyal in Pulwama attack, and cleared SSC exams & interview and is all set to serve the Indian army with pride. For this, she sacrificed her job in a Noida-based MNC.

The extract here is to ***become responsible for your past, present, and future YOU***. It is only you who choose to work in a certain company, it is you who choose to do a particular college to study. It is only you who decided. I also agree that the power of choice is a luxury which we all may not have in the same amount as deciding which college and course to join, mainly influenced by people, and in particular, family around us. It was, of course, you who choose a girlfriend or a partner for you and later on break up or get divorced.
And even then, you put the blame on your partners the situations and other craps.

If you ever find yourselves in such a situation, I would strongly recommend you read the book "Start with Why," written by Simon Sinek. It is such an amazing book that brought out the best in me and still I carry the experience in my hand even when I have finished reading it.

Those who belong to the breed of achievers and champions were not told by their family or friends to do and love what brought them the vast richness of success. It was themselves who decided to pursue that path of their love, the path where they belong, and the path which they will never regret after being beaten down. And, if you think they had the luxury of power of choice and the entire situation in their life was *perfect*, then my friend, you need to re-think. It was them who underwent the most robust phase, right from meeting both the ends meet. They even didn't have the luxury of two full meals and sound sleep. For many of them, you know had to spend sleepless nights on streets to get ready for the next day championship match. Many of them had to sell newspapers to make both ends meet. Many of them had to study under streetlamps to complete their assignments.

This inscribes the first state of mind, ***the state of responsibility.*** And if you carefully observe any known achiever, you can very well connect. Also, for all the things that you have achieved, however microscopic or humungous it may be, you will realize that you achieved in this very state of mind.

Once you achieve this state of mind, you will dive further into the second state of mind, i.e. ***The state of attention,*** which means you choose what to attend to and what not to. For example, have you ever observed your hot cup of coffee or tea getting cold as you forgot to sip because you were so engrossed in reading or watching something? Have you ever entered into a room but forgot why did you even enter the room? Or something similar like forgetting car keys or phone or even the car itself where you have parked? Or have you ever worn a different pair of socks? I did that, and one of my close, I mean very close girlfriend noticed and then suddenly all burst into a fit of laughter. I was so prepared and engrossed for the meeting that was to take place that I wore a different pair of socks.

This all happens due to either lack of attention or due to complete attention to an activity that makes the other activity of sipping through your coffee virtually invisible. So, this journey can only be fruitful if you are paying attention. If you have on boarded this journey just for the heck of reading or serving this book as a sedative or sleep-inducing agent, then my dear champions this journey or any other book is not going to help you.

So, let us sip a cup of coffee or juice and take a break. Just go out, have a walk outside, listen to your favorite song, or just chat with your love only if you are lucky enough to have one. Meanwhile, let me continue to do what I love to do.

Did you take a break? If not, I would strongly recommend it, and if you can`t resist reading the book, I have a lot more in store for you.

After you have decided & achieved the 2nd state, i.e., the state of attention. It is time now not to dive but to give you wings to fly high in the form of the third state of mind, i.e., ***The state of Neurogenesis***. To make this crystal clear, I would like to share the extract of a superb TED talk by Sandrine Thuret at BCG London.

Can we, as adults, grow new nerve cells? There's still some confusion about that question, as this is a fairly new field of research. For example, when Sandrine was talking to one of her colleagues, Robert, who is an oncologist, and he was telling her, "Sandrine, this is puzzling. Some of my patients that have been told they are cured of their cancer still develop symptoms of depression." And she responded to him, "Well, from my point of view, that makes sense. The drug you give to your patients that stops the cancer cells from multiplying also stops the newborn neurons from being generated in their brain." And then Robert looked at her like she was crazy and said, "But Sandrine, these are adult patients -- adults do not grow new nerve cells." And much to his surprise, she said, "Well, actually, we do." And this is a phenomenon that we call neurogenesis.

https://en.wikipedia.org/wiki/Neurogenesis
Neurogenesis is the process by which nervous system cells, the neurons, are produced by neural stem cells (NSC)s. It occurs in all species of animals except the Porifera (sponges) and placozoans. Types of NSCs include neuroepithelial cells (NECs), radial glial cells (RGCs), basal progenitors (BPs), intermediate neuronal precursors (INP)s, subventricular zone astrocytes, and subgranular zone radial astrocytes, among others. Neurogenesis is most active during embryonic development and is responsible for producing all the various types of neurons of the organism but continues throughout adult life in a variety of organisms. Once born, neurons do not divide, and many will live the lifespan of the animal.

So why are these new neurons important, and what are their functions? First, we know that they're important for learning and memory. And in the lab, Sandrine and her team have shown that if we block the ability of the adult brain to produce new neurons in the hippocampus, then we block certain memory abilities. And this is especially new and true for spatial recognition -- so like, how you navigate your way in the city.

We are still learning a lot, and neurons are not only crucial for memory capacity, but also for the quality of the memory. And they will have been helpful to add time to our memory, and they will help differentiate very similar memories, like how do you find the bike that you park at the station every day in the same area, but in a slightly different position?

So, collectively, now we think we have enough evidence to say that neurogenesis is a target of choice if we want to improve memory formation or mood, or even prevent the decline associated with aging, or associated with stress. So, the next question is: can we control neurogenesis? The answer is yes. And we are now going to do a little quiz. I'm going to give you a set of behaviors and activities, and you tell me if you think they will increase neurogenesis or if they will decrease neurogenesis. Are we ready? OK, let's take off.

1. What about learning? Increasing? Yes. Learning will increase the production of these new neurons.
2. How about stress? Yes, stress will decrease the production of new neurons in the hippocampus.
3. How about sleep deprivation? Indeed, it will decrease neurogenesis.
4. How about sex? Oh, wow! Yes, you are right it will increase the production of new neurons. However, it's all about balance here. We don't want to fall in a situation about too much sex leading to sleep deprivation.
5. How about getting older? So, the neurogenesis rate will decrease as we get older, but it is still occurring.
6. And then finally, how about playing cricket or snooker? I will let you judge that one by yourself.

So, activity impacts neurogenesis, but that's not all. What you eat will have an effect on the production of new neurons in the hippocampus. So, here is what Sandrine and her team has a sample of the diet -- of nutrients that have been shown to have efficacy. And I'm just going to point a few out to you: Calorie restriction of 20 to 30 percent will increase neurogenesis. Intermittent fasting -- spacing the time between your meals -- will increase neurogenesis. Intake of flavonoids, which are contained in dark chocolate or blueberries, will increase neurogenesis. Omega-3 fatty acids, present in fatty fish, like salmon, will increase the production of these new neurons. Conversely, a diet rich in high saturated fat, will hurt neurogenesis. Ethanol -- intake of alcohol -- will decrease neurogenesis. However, not everything is lost; resveratrol, which is contained in red wine, has been shown to promote the survival of these new neurons. So next time you are at a dinner party, you might want to reach for this possibly "neurogenesis-neutral" drink.

And then finally, let me point out the last one -- a quirky one by Sandrine. So Japanese groups are fascinated with food textures, and they have shown that actually, soft diet impairs neurogenesis, as opposed to food that requires mastication -- chewing -- or crunchy food.

So, the extract is: ***The State of Neurogenesis*** plays a vital role in learning.

The state of Neuroplasticity

Now, as you are aware of the beauty of neurogenesis, let us get the ball rolling for the next critical department of the brain, i.e., ***Neuroplasticity***. By this time, you must have realized that I am a huge fan of

TED talks. I will again take the help of a few of the finest talks by Lara Boyd and Josh Kaufman.

Have you ever heard of this term before? If the answer is yes, I have another question as to how much do you know about it? And, even if the answer is on the flip side, no need to worry. I will assist you to completely and clearly understand it with an actionable plan towards it.

https://en.wikipedia.org/wiki/Neuroplasticity
Neuroplasticity, also known as brain plasticity, or neural plasticity, is the ability of the brain to change continuously throughout an individual's life, e.g., brain activity associated with a given function can be transferred to a different location, the proportion of grey matter can change, and synapses may strengthen or weaken over time. The aim of neuroplasticity is to optimize the neural networks during phylogenesis, ontogeny, and physiological learning, as well as after a brain injury. Research in the latter half of the 20th century showed that many aspects of the brain can be altered (or are "plastic") even through adulthood. However, the developing brain exhibits a higher degree of plasticity than the adult brain.

I will insist you all to direct your attention to the below-mentioned lines:

Study WHAT & HOW you learn best. You have to PRACTICE. And become aware of what your brain requires.

These lines have their roots to my strongest belief that everyone`s learning style and type is unique, and we can`t have one size fits all approach. But contrary to my belief, this is what is practically practiced. The greatest challenge is to become aware what method and style of your learning do your brain accepts easily and efficiently. Getting back to the question when Rahul (the young me 12 years old) had taken the pledge to top the school in a year and the current situation, then you are already aware. How could a failure drastically change and take on a journey to become a topper?

Interestingly the challenge for him was not WHAT to study but rather HOW to study. And taking a closer look WHY he should even study. He accidentally found the answer to his WHY in the form of making his parents proud and to the atonement of hurting them by not studying.

Simon Sinek, author of a marvelous book, "Start with Why," has nicely put the answer to the WHY of everything. That's the epicenter of all the great work and successful companies and individuals. If you look closely at the life of any champion, you will realize that they all had one thing in common. They had a very strong WHY. After they found their answer to the WHY, nature magically gives the answer to the HOW and finding the WHAT just becomes as easy as cutting a cake with a sword.

If you take a look at current educational institutions, they all sadly focus only on WHAT. The most important factors for learning, WHY & HOW is seldom focused on. And this is the problem with the current education system. As responsible for future, we the trainers, teachers, and all those involved in imparting the most valuable gift of nature, the priceless possession of all with the greatest ROI (Return On Investment) against any investment: ***Knowledge & Learning,*** should focus on trying to develop the mental faculties of learners which enables them to uncover the answers to WHY, HOW & WHAT. And in the process, we must realize that there is nothing (at least in the learning & knowledge domain) available as one size fits all approach. You should also put up a question as to why you should read this book or any other book. If you don't have the answer to this question, you will not be able to extract what the book promises to gift you. So, let's get back to one of the states of mind or one of the departments as I better called it in the previous sections.

Neuroplasticity can be observed at multiple scales, from microscopic changes in individual neurons to larger-scale changes such as cortical remapping in response to injury. Behavior, environmental stimuli, thought, and emotions may also cause neuroplastic change through activity-dependent plasticity, which has significant implications for healthy development, learning, memory, and recovery from brain damage. At the single-cell level, synaptic plasticity refers to changes in the connections between neurons, whereas non-synaptic plasticity refers to changes in their intrinsic excitability.

Several studies have linked meditation practice to differences in cortical thickness or density of gray matter. One of the most well-known studies to demonstrate this was led by Sara Lazar, from Harvard University in 2000. Richard Davidson, a neuroscientist at the University of Wisconsin, has led experiments in cooperation with the Dalai Lama on the effects of meditation on the brain. His results suggest that long-term or short-term practice of meditation results in different levels of activity in brain regions associated with such qualities as attention, anxiety, depression, fear, anger, and the ability of the body to heal itself. These functional changes may be caused by changes in the physical structure of the brain.

Aerobic exercise promotes adult neurogenesis by increasing the production of neurotrophic factors (compounds that promote growth or survival of neurons), such as brain-derived neurotrophic factor (BDNF), insulin-like growth factor 1 (IGF-1), and vascular endothelial growth factor (VEGF). Exercise-induced neurogenesis in the hippocampus is associated with measurable improvements in spatial memory. Consistent aerobic exercise over several months induces marked clinically significant improvements in executive function (i.e., the "cognitive control" of behavior) and increased gray matter volume in multiple brain regions, particularly those that give rise to cognitive control.

The brain structures that show the greatest improvements in gray matter volume in response to aerobic exercise are the prefrontal cortex and hippocampus. Moderate improvements are seen in the anterior cingulate cortex, parietal cortex, cerebellum, caudate nucleus, and nucleus accumbens. Higher physical fitness scores (measured by VO_2 max) are associated with better executive function, faster processing speed, and the greater volume of the hippocampus, caudate nucleus, and nucleus accumbens.

Human echolocation is a learned ability for humans to sense their environment from echoes. This ability is used by some blind people to navigate their environment and sense their surroundings in detail. Studies in 2010 and 2011 using functional magnetic resonance imaging techniques have shown that parts of the brain associated with visual processing are adapted for the new skill of echolocation. Studies with blind patients, for example, suggest that the click-echoes heard by these patients were processed by brain regions devoted to vision rather than audition.

Neuroplasticity is most active in childhood as a part of normal human development and can also be seen as an especially important mechanism for children in terms of risk and resiliency. Trauma is considered a great risk as it negatively affects many areas of the brain and puts a strain on the sympathetic nervous system from constant activation. Trauma thus alters the brain's connections such that children who have experienced trauma may be hyper-vigilant or overly aroused. However, a child's brain can cope with these adverse effects through the actions of neuroplasticity.

There are many examples of neuroplasticity in human development. In an article written by Justine Ker and Stephen Nelson," the effects of musical training on neuroplasticity" is looked at. Musical training is a form of experience-dependent plasticity. This is when changes in the brain occur based on experiences that are unique to an individual. Examples of this are learning multiple languages, playing a sport, doing theatre, etc. A study done by Hyde in 2009 showed that changes in the brain of children could be seen in as little as 15 months of musical training. Ker and Nelson suggest this degree of plasticity in the brains of children can "help provide a form of intervention for children with developmental disorders and neurological diseases."

The beneficial effect of multilingualism on people's behavior and cognition are well-known nowadays. Numerous studies have shown that people who study more than one language have better cognitive functions and flexibilities than people who only speak one language. Bilinguals are found to have longer attention spans, stronger organization and analyzation skills, and a better theory of mind than monolinguals. Researchers have found that the effect of multilingualism on better cognition is due to neuroplasticity.

In one prominent study, neurolinguists used **voxel-based morphometry (VBM) method** to visualize the structural plasticity of brains in healthy monolinguals and bilinguals. They first investigated the differences in density of grey and white matter between two groups and found the relationship between brain structure and age of language acquisition. The results showed that grey-matter density in the inferior parietal cortex for multilingual individuals was significantly greater than monolingual individuals. The researchers also found that early bilinguals had a greater density of grey matter relative to late bilinguals in the same region. The inferior parietal cortex is a brain region highly associated with language learning, which corresponds to the VBM result of the study.

Recent studies have also found that learning multiple languages not only re-structures the brain but also boosts the brain's capacity for plasticity. A recent study found that multilingualism not only affects the grey matter but also the white matter of the brain. White matter is made up of myelinated axons that are greatly associated with ***learning and communication***. Neurolinguists used a diffusion tensor imaging (DTI) scanning method to determine the white matter intensity between monolinguals and bilinguals. Increased myelinations in white matter tracts were found in bilingual individuals who actively use both languages in everyday life. The demand for handling more than one language requires more efficient connectivity within the brain and grey matter, which resulted in greater white matter density for multilingual people.

The State of Assumed learning

What can you learn from water? Think deeply. Let me also help you. May be transparency or to flow so that you don't become stagnant. What can you learn from a table? Think. May be we can learn solidarity or keeping yourself grounded or having a good posture with the help of exercise.

Look around where you are sitting. Take any 5 objects around you and break it. Oh! If you really do it, your mom or wife, or else your husband or father will hang you upside down. Hehe!

By breaking, I mean here to ask the question as to what you can learn from each of the objects. I would really love it if you could spare some time to do this activity before further reading. I insist, please do it.

You will be amazed to see the amazing answers that your mental faculties will provide you with. Here you also used one of the important principles of learning, i.e., ***Autosuggestion,*** discussed in the upcoming paragraphs. Just by being in the ***state of assumed learning***, by non-living things, if you can learn so much, imagine the vast & massive amounts of knowledge you will be able to unfold from your mentors, Teachers. I will also tell you one secret. You can learn from just observing people and objects around you. That is how purely talented actors learn and perform their finest acts. For example, Nawazuddin Siddiqui, & Yashpal Sharma, both of my most favorite actors, have learnt in these lines. They have revealed that their observation is the secret behind their classy acting. But the observation can only be fruitful when you acquire the ***state of assumed learning***.

So, the next time you go for a walk, remember to keep your mind in this state and let it magically work for you. If you don't believe me, I would urge all of you to go out for a walk and try to keep your state of mind, as stated above. Though it requires practice to be in such a state, I assure you that you will be amazed to see the results from the very first act of trial and it will exponentially upsurge your belief about this state of mind. This state of mind deliberately leads us to another very critical aspect of the state of mind.

The State of Curiosity

Do you ever wonder that questions are powerful? The quality of questions one asks can be well served as a yardstick of intelligence of a person. Do you know why the sky is blue? Why is it that water can make a paper wet, but mercury droplets can`t, though both of them are liquids? You may get to the answers by any medium, like the internet, books, teachers, or others.

But you will reach the answers only when you are curious enough to know it. You can apply this state of mind to any field – academics, sports, arts, music, etc.

you can see wonders happening through this state of mind. All the biggest inventions have their roots in such a state of mind. And, I am sure you will agree with me that these inventions would have been far from reach without this state of mind. And this is a universal thumb rule for all. This is such a hat that can be called as *one size fits all*. Only the implementation would differ but not the roots. Let us take an example here.

Their names are Bhavik & Bhushita, 12 and 15 years old, respectively. I happened to meet them luckily through Linkedin contacts. They, being at such an age, have got thoughts much mature than their counterparts. They formed Samvedna, a small brain-child of these two sweet ***kidopreneurs,*** who intend to impact the lives of the have-nots of the society, especially kids who are deprived of exposure and resources.

They used to play Ludo, chess, and other indoor games with their mom at the tender age of 7. Soon they became interested in chess and became curious. So, from the state of joy, their mind transmuted to ***the state of curiosity.*** After playing just for fun for a few years, they developed such interest and curiosity in the field of chess that they soon began to take professional training and do wonders. Their curiosity gifted them with trophies, medals, and accolades widely. They now stand as state-level chess champions.

Their accolades include:

1. Bronze in Commonwealth games.
2. Sustained in Top-20 in National under 7 held at Kolkata.
3. 3rd prize in IIFL Regional qualifications and was selected to represent Delhi State in IFFL Mumbai Chess Tournament.
4. 2nd Best Delhi Female Players' prize in All India Open Chess Tournament.
5. Best Under 10 Prize in IIFL Mumbai Chess Tournament.
6. 2nd Best Delhi Female Players' prize in Sameen Singh Chess Tournament held at Amritsar.
7. 3rd in Delhi State Women Championship.
8. 2nd in Delhi State under 13 categories.
9. 3rd in Ambheesh Sinha Chess Tournament (Under 1400 category)
10. Participation in London Chess Classics, Representing India.
11. Participation in Teplice International Open, Representing India.
12. Represented Delhi State in National under 13, held in Jalandhar.

It was fascinating to understand the software of their brains. Let me share some insights into these two bright young minds and how do they think.

Today, they owe chess a significant time for its contribution in shaping them into the confident and resilient individuals that they are today. Sports have nurtured them and inculcated a bunch of essential life skills that have made them thought leaders. Looking back now, it is quite surprising for them to think about the journey they have had with chess. From just a board game to how the 64 squares became an integral part of their lifestyle.

8 years down the line, they thought, the chess pieces were plastic figurines and today, they consider them like family! Spending 8 hours a day in front of the chessboard, playing games for hours at a stretch, chess has ignited the logical side of their brain and encouraged them to think beyond boundaries. They are blessed with highly supportive family members and teachers who continue to fuel the engine of their dreams.

The crossroads came when they stepped into middle school. As academic pressure incessantly kept building, they had to make a choice between academics and sports. Their family didn't want them to leave education at such a tender age, and at that point, they agreed with it. They gave chess a break and began focusing on their books. However, little did they know that their passion for this game had already entered their bloodstream? The spirit of sportsmanship besieged their heart, knocked at their ribs. Sports had become their lifestyle.

That's when they decided to give back to the game that had been uplifting their character and personality and teaching them more than the books. They wanted to ignite this passion into others, who aren't well off. That's how they came up with 'Samvedna' - which means empathy. Through this foundation, they organized a chess tournament in December at the Banyan Tree School New Delhi. They garnered an audience of 250+ players across NCR, and the event was further endorsed by Mr. Gautam Gambhir as well as the sports minister of the country, Mr. Kiren Rijiju. They used the funds generated through this event to open classes in 2 Slums of Delhi. They further hope to touch more lives soon and continue to serve society, forever and always. In the end, as they said - "Sports is like medicine to the body and music to mind, it polishes our attitude, making us humble and kind."

I was fortunate enough to meet them and form an association to take our common pledge of impacting lives via good cause that includes sports and games that imprint life skills like leadership, problem-solving, teamwork, planning, resilience, creativity, and the list goes on.

The state of Having a WHY/Purpose

Have you ever asked a question of never-ending motivation?
As earlier described about having a purpose behind your action, has the ability to transform your desires into physical results. For this principle I will just like to share few examples that will make it vivid what this state means and how you can benefit from it. A lot of people whom I meet have asked me as to how I am always motivated? What is the secret behind my never ending motivation? If you are also keen to know the answer to this question. Then this is absolutely for you.

All the successful organization, by working on this principle has achieved enormous riches. The best one among all I must mention, recent one that I have already mentioned about a resilient woman , Nitika Kaul, who lost her husband, Major Vibhuti Shankar Dhoundiyal in Pulwama Attack, and cleared SSC exams & interview and is all set to serve the Indian army with pride. Can you see the strong 'why' here behind her efforts to achieve this feat? It was of course her hard labor and efforts for the preparation for the exams, but her efforts were backed by a strong 'why' that led her to a never-ending motivation. The strong 'why' made her persevere efforts, despite being in such a state of mind of losing her husband.

Apple, the brand about which so much has been already written. I would like to share just the difference that it creates with a strong purpose in the market. And it is evident from its logo, i.e., think different. And people get associated with the 'Why' of the rather than 'what' of the apple that is served by its product. People get so connected that they are ready to stand in long queues to get a smart phone on its launch on a higher price despite the fact that it will soon be available at their doorstep at a relatively much economical price. The 'why' of the Brand Apple keeps them glued with every new launch. They want to be the earliest ones to experience the magic of being different.

Then there is a 17-year-old Rahul, a younger version of mine (remember being detached helps me to write without any bias) who learnt this principle with three of his biggest mistakes in life. I must share this as whatever I have learnt I realized that experiential learning is the best form of learning as also advised by Swami Vivekananda.

I would like to again put up one of the phrases mentioned earlier in the book,

"If you are going through hell, keep going. Why would you stop in hell?"

Over the years after struggling and making mistakes, he wondered - ***Is crisis an indication to something great?*** This question was answered as a big YES when he saw the things unfold in unimaginable positive outlook. And I am really glad that that this somehow, the blessings of creative faculties of my mind enabled me to bring this forward. One should always be ready to firstly, accept his or her mistakes and secondly to act on those mistakes to turn the mistakes into blessings.

To prove this, I am going to share with you the top three mistakes, *(among a number of mistakes that I did)*, I have made in my professional career and also the learning or rather learnings that I took from them.

The very first one, early in his career, dates back to the college days in 2009 that he did out of his curiosity and also family needs then. He left his college, in Delhi University, (one of the most reputed college in Delhi) while going for one of his chemistry exams. While he was in the bus on the way to the college, some questions popped out:

1. Why is he pursuing this particular course? (Chemistry Hons.)
2. Is he happy doing this course?
3. How would he take care of my family as this course would enable him to earn not before 2012 after he completes his Graduation? And

the present situation then demands him to start earning as early as possible.

4. Does he see himself associated with the profession and the type of course chosen even after 10 to 20 years?

These questions besides others led him to a decision to leave the course then and there and he returned back home without appearing for the exams. (Though it seems ridiculous to do so and he was presented with whatever stern dialogues his well-wishers could gift him. The list included parents, good friends and teachers. Abuses and every alibi & what not that also to an extent led him to depression or his inability to deal with the decision and its after-effects).

This may resemble to the after-effects during COVID-19 era when we all have seen mass exodus of labourers from UP, Bihar and other adjoining states soon after the announcement of the lockdown to curb the deadly pandemic. The decision maker that our PM made for our benefit but couldn't think of the aftershocks that was bound to come.

Learnings for the mistake:

1. Always ***start with a strong Wh***y. Be it profession, education or any decision.
2. Decision making, its impact & the importance of definiteness of Decision and its purpose.
3. Love what you do & Do what you love. (Don't wait to discover your *Passion*, have a craftsmen mindset. Make the things at hand as

best as you can even if you are not passionate.)
4. If you are not happy doing a thing, it is not for you.
5. Be decisive but with poise.
6. Beware of Dogmatization. (To believe on facts rather than opinions).

Secondly, while working with one of the brands in Noida, he couldn't control his reaction to reply to one of the wrong statements of his boss, and he left the company that very moment.

Learning from the mistakes:

1. You always have the luxury of choosing your reaction to a particular situation and behaviors of others. Others should not have the power to make you react a certain way. So, it is up to you to choose your reaction or to better put it ***he learnt to act/not act rather than react.***
2. Patience
3. Stress- Management.

Thirdly, with one of the projects, way back when I had left the college, I suffered huge losses in terms of money, time & friendships. The major reasons for failure were, misunderstanding the **timing**. Lack of definite plan, lack of monetization, neglecting the importance of contracts and documentation. Poorly managing funds and others.

Learning from the mistakes:

1. Work-Life Balance
2. Attention to details
3. Importance of Documentation & Contracts
4. Financial Literacy

The essence of this discussion takes us to the Why of everything. Each of the mistakes missed the why factor. The moment he learnt the art of having a why behind almost everything, mistakes gradually decreased, and this became a principle in his life. This finally galvanized into a very important state of mind i.e., ***the state of having a why/Purpose.***

So, creating a zone inside the brain that has ***the 7 states of mind,*** can serve as an asset of incomparable value. It makes you immune to failure & fear. And if you have bought insurance anytime in life, I must tell you that you have automobile, health and other types of insurance but you don't have any insurance for the brain yet.

But there is some good news for you all. By developing these 7 states of mind, you actually develop **insurance for your brain** for which the premium is not much as compared to the ROI (return on investment it provides). It serves as an insurance against your failure, fear, discouragement, criticism and gives you a never-ending motivation to pursue your goals. And it is very easy to remember. You just need to remember & practice ***RANNACH,*** that's all.

Principle 6: The Zorro Circle

Have you heard of the movie "The Mask of Zorro?" Whether you have heard it or not doesn't make a difference, but the principle is so effective that it has helped us complete the journey of writing this book for you all. I have been thinking all my growing years how someone writes such humungous number of words in books. Don't they get bored? I was really interested in writing a book to share my thoughts with everyone from early childhood but it was crazy to think to start writing. More than crazy it was so horrendous.

I got the solution when I first came to know about the Zorro Circle. I must say it is so simple yet so powerful that it can be applied to so many fields. Let me first list the fields or actionable areas where you can apply this principle.

1. Education & Learning.
2. Personal Financial Management
3. De-cluttering your house.
4. Stress management and so on.

And the list will be endless. We will restrict ourselves to its application in learning. And once you master this art, you can apply this in any field. But first of all let us apply HEAL here to know the background of this principle. This has also been well explained by Shawn Achor in his book, "The Happiness Advantage".

Several years ago, movie theatres were rocked by the film "The Mask of Zorro" featuring Anthony Hopkins, Antonio Banderas and Catherine Zeta Jones. The anecdote of Zorro is also well known who was a masked champion of the people who fought against official corruption in the early 19th Century.

We meet Alejandro Murrieta at the very start of the film who was a young man and wanted to settle the scores for the death of his brother and wanted justice for his village. This would have been possible by fighting against a humungous army. Unfortunately, he is undisciplined and untrained, Alejandro couldn't achieve progress and in anguish over his inability to defeat the army, he turns to drinking.

After initial despair, Alejandro meets Don Diego AKA Zorro. Don decided to train him. Alejandro tries hard in the beginning but he's imprudent and uncontrolled. Subsequently, Zorro introduces Alejandro to the "Training Circle".

Let us learn about the training circle and this is very relevant to be applied to our learning & training methodologies:

1. *The Training circle is a circle filled with obstacles and ropes in which he will be educated to fight.*
2. *Zorro explains that Alejandro's whole world will be that circle.*
3. *As soon as Alejandro's skill with the sword improves and he gains some control with practice, he will move on to a new circle.*

So the basic idea of the Zorro Circle is not take a task as whole at once, but to encircle a significant small area in the entire task. Once you conquer this circle and gain control then you broaden or expand your circle. This also resembles by one of the concepts in the book "Zero to One" where the authors Peter Thiel & Blake Masters puts this fact to start a business with a large share of small market. The large market will be the entire task or market to be captured and small market would be the Zorro Circle in that context. He says to first capture a large share of the small market i.e. the Zorro Circle and then you expand.

The Ideas behind the Zorro Circle must be understood as:

1) You are able to take control of the situation by starting with small, manageable steps.
2) Research shows that we're happier and able to perform at a higher level when we feel that we're in control of a situation.

3) Our brain if overtaken by fear and stress which significantly reduces our efficiency when the task is huge and we lose the feeling of control and influence.
4) Once you master one particular area, you can expand that mastery outward.
5) Keep escalating outward your Zorro Circle until you've achieved your goal.

The next question is how can you apply this in your lives? I am sure it is evident yet I will present some examples that will help you to apply this principle effectively.

For example let us look at our personal finance. And how can we forget credit card bills or debts that have become a part of life. It is a vicious circle that eats your earning and savings as well. In order to control debts by significantly reducing them or eradicating them entirely, let us start by drawing a Zorro circle around your debts. And focus mostly on reducing it. Unless you significantly reduce your debts over a period of say, 3 to 6 months or more, don't focus on any other areas of personal finance like investing, savings.

Also form a discipline by avoiding extra expenses of socializing and weekend enjoyments along with shopping. Once you have significantly reduced your debts and you have gained control on debts you can expand your Zorro Circle. So guys what are you waiting for, go ahead and apply by drawing a Zorro circle today. Action speaks louder than words.

More than reading the book, taking action will bring a change in your lives.

You can efficiently apply Zorro circle in your health. To start with it is very important to be mentally fit along with physical health. Draw a circle around gaining control on your stress first. Look for the things that increase your stress levels. Try to inculcate healthy habits that reduce your stress. You may start by getting spiritual, connecting with nature besides other significant methods of meditation, music, reading a book or giving at least an hour a day to your favorite hobby. You will see soon reduction in stress levels. Then you may gradually expand the Zorro circle around other aspects of mental and physical health like yoga, physical exercise.

In case you suddenly decide to be healthy and reduce weight, usually it is evident by various researches where people join gym at the beginning of the year full of enthusiasm, soon asking the gym owners to refund their amount within few weeks or months because they lose enthusiasm and get busy in other significant tasks.

With the Covid`19 pandemic, it made us realize strongly that health is the most sought after asset for human beings and all the things can wait. With more than 3 million deaths world over and over 2 lakhs death (as on 29th April 2020) and many praying to get well and back in their lives, it is evident that health can`t be compensated by millions of dollars or strong army base. Health has been the most significant asset and will continue to be. Any investment towards health is worth it. There can`t be a strong reminder to change our unhealthy habits and move towards healthier habits.

Principle 7: Tetris Effect

Now as you are aware of neuroplasticity, it will be like a cakewalk for you. It can also help us to magnify our learning process. I learnt about this in the same book, mentioned for the earlier Principle of Zorro Circle. Let us make it very simple to understand. ***The Principle of Repetition***. This is a very powerful concept. Can you now guess it? I think yes. You must have got a hint. It has very pivotal role to play in the process of learning.

How do you become an expert in certain skill? Or to be put it further, can you think about a skill that you have mastered in the past? Ever wondered, how did you do that?

You have devoted a significant number of hours to that skill. An obvious answer but it has something to do with understanding of human brain function. It is as simple as it is written as ***repetition***. Let us now understand it by gaining an insight by what happens with our brain every time we repeat something.

Tetris Effect derives its name from the game Tetris. If you remember, you may have played it. Before Xbox and other sophisticated video games that we see today, we had hand video games back in 1990`s where we were supposed to arrange falling rectangular boxes into structures at the bottom that could fit in so that we could make points. The challenge was to modify the shape horizontally or vertically and move it to the left or right before it hit the bottom. That was the game. An interesting experiment was performed by Psychiatry Department of the *Harvard Medical School*.

It included 27 respondents who were asked to play this game regularly for 3 days and that too for long hours. The respondents were paid significant amount for playing it. And why won`t anyone play it? Of course even if I would have been asked, I too would have played. What can be better than the feeling of being paid for playing a game? Moving on after some days, these respondents were asked few questions whose results were surprising. Many of them said that they can now see Tetris shapes falling from the sky. One even said that every time he sees a building, he thinks about which shape would fill the gap between two buildings so that it can become an unbroken horizontal line.

The results were inferred by researchers that by playing long hours of the game, the respondents had developed and connected new neural pathways due to which they were able to observe Tetris in real lives. This phenomenon was named as ***The Tetris Effect***.

So the good news is, with the knowledge of this effect we can wire our minds the way we want simply by repeating related activities significant number of times. Say for example you find it difficult to handle stress. And it is natural and you are no different. So let us put this effect to use. Wondering how? It is very simple by repeatedly doing activities that counter stress like meditation or physical exercise. My secret for handling stress relies on the technique on *Box Breathing*. Learn about this technique in a superb book, *The Unbeatable Mind, by Mark Divine*.

Let us say whenever you find yourselves in stressful situation you should think about your favorite song for a few minutes or drink water. Pick any technique that you like as long as it proves effective to you and you do it repeatedly. Over a period of time you will have significantly developed neural pathways of handling stressful situations and you will gradually become better at this. Another example can be a bad habit like smoking. Can you connect now? Despite realizing the dangers, why do we smoke? The answer is very simple. By repeating smoking a significant number of times we have created neural pathways of craving for a smoke. So you can also use this effect to develop a new habit or put a curb on a bad one. This has to be backed by consistent efforts of altering your smoke craving with some healthy habits. Think about it.

If one reads this one Shloka —

क्लैब्यंमास्मगमःपार्थनैतत्त्वय्युपपद्यते।क्षुद्रंहृदयदौर्बल्यंत्यक्त्वोत्ति ष्ठपरंतप॥

— one gets all the merits of reading the entire Gita; for in this one Shloka lies imbedded the whole Message of the Gita

-Swami Vivekananda

Chapter 6: A Confluence with the epic BHAGWADGITA

First of all, I am, so blessed to have met such a divine book or a journey that is the best that I could ever read. And I thank the almighty, my parents, my friends or anyone whom I have touched upon in life or vice-versa, that created a situation that led me to read the epic BHAGVAD GITA. I feel so tiny to even take the name, but I can`t control the temptation to share with you what my conscience allowed me to extract from the book.

https://en.wikipedia.org/wiki/Bhagavad_Gita
The first lady of my life, i.e. my mother once told me that she had already read Bhagvad Gita. To my surprise, she also exclaimed that, you just can`t read it like any other book. You have the luxury to choose to read any book. But the case is slightly different here. As once you are on a humane path, the book itself chooses the soul that must read the book. I didn't believe her at all at first.

I started reading the book on my choice. Soon I found that magically the book slipped, and I was entangled into the worldly occupancies. Later on, when I was in self-realization mode, probably two years after, I recollected the words of my mother and I was astonished to find that she was absolutely correct.

I just couldn't read or complete the Bhagvad Gita journey despite trying to start it several times. So now the time finally came and here it is.

So, I am sure many of you have gone through it already, but everyone has a different interpretation. Whether you have had a chance to read it or not, I am certain that you will benefit from this.

Let me take you on an epic journey and I am delighted to share whatever I could extract.
According to the exegesis scholar Robert Minor, the Gita is "probably the most translated of any Asian text". Bhagvad Gita is considered to be 5000 years old with 18 chapters explained with the help of 700 verses.

It may be divided to into 3 broad sections:

1. Chapter 1 to 6 : Karma Yoga
2. Chapter 7 to 12 : Bhakti Yoga
3. Chapter 13 to 18 : Jnana Yoga

I would like to take you on a journey that I am sure will give you to the answers to questions that makes much of *NOISE* in our heads and has provided me the real insights of how the world works.

It has helped me to grow and provide a clear path.

Relationships – A blessing by the almighty, transformed into curse by us.

Let us start with the most interesting above all i.e. relationships. After suffering through around 11 break-ups and some of which I even don't remember, I was so depressed, and the failures of relationships led me to believe that I am not good at all with relationships. I understand that this is hard to believe and it's a long list. Everyone once in a lifetime becomes anti-parent. I also believed once that my parents are my enemy and would take revenge once I grow and will be able to stand on my own.

Have you ever found yourselves in such a situation when you are against your own parents with respect to career, love affairs, finance etc.? Have you ever found your best of the friends becoming a cause for your suffering? I am sure you must have been in such situations and many of you may be struggling even now.

Do you ever wonder why does this happen? To better understand this, I would urge all of you to remember your recent cause of pain due to your relationships. Moreover, it doesn't mean only your better half. I mean your bosses, parents, siblings, friends and you may have a long list to remember.

Why did it happen? You think the person was wrong and he/she didn't get what you tried to make them understand.

Isn't it true that our protection, solutions to problems, financial goals, health and overall emotional well-being linked to relationships? After all we all are social animals and after the advent of technology it has become many times difficult to maintain healthy relationships.

There are three things that happen naturally in your relationships and the interesting part is that we don't need to do anything to achieve those. Can you think of few things? I leave that up to you.

Those three things I personally have found are:

1. Friction
2. Confusion
3. Misunderstanding

Everything else requires your efforts. Taking guidance from the epic Bhagvad Gita, and also after experiencing the benefits, I am taking you for a ride.

What is the foundation of all our relationships?
All the relationships are based on ***expectation***. How a wife wants a husband to be? A person who can provide her with all the joy that she wants. Parents want their children to listen to them. They raise children with the expectation that their children will support when they themselves grow old. How a wife should be? One who is dedicated to the husband? Friends expect to be supported when they are in need. Wives expect their husbands to take care of them with respect to finance, emotional support etc.

And you will say you already know this. What is the big deal here? And there is nothing wrong with this.
You water plants & trees with the expectation of fruits and shadow.

A human is able to love only those who fulfill their expectations and the interesting fact is that expectation has to a ***nature to change*** infinitely over time. Is it possible to touch the same water droplets of a flowing river twice? Absolutely not.

Trying to fulfill expectations is exactly the case mentioned here. So, deliberately you try to achieve what is against the nature of law. This gives rise to the struggle in relationships.

Diving further deep, all relationships have set boundaries which altogether defines the relationship. e.g., when you have a husband-wife relationship, the partner is expected to maintain a distance from the opposite sex, expected to dedicate a desired quality time. When you are siblings, you make interesting boundaries as to not share the *secrets* & *mischievous acts* with parents so that you didn't get a hard bashing. Whosoever breaks the boundaries loses trust with his counterpart and imbibes a pain in his/her heart.

Though, setting boundaries is a very good way to have trustworthy relationships, yet it gives rise to immense pain and sets our life towards the path of struggle and self-wars within.

So, what is the right way? Do we even have a way by which we can have healthy relationships? The good news is yes. And the most interesting fact it is far easier than setting boundaries method.
Are you ready to accept? But before that I would like to ask you to think of the quality of relationships you have with your parents, elders, friends, girlfriend or boyfriend, husband or wife and whoever you may think of.

The key to healthy relationships is ***Independence & Acceptance***. Imagine how you feel when a career choice is not discussed but imposed on you by parents. This hurts our independence. How about a fantastic idea that you present to your boss, but you are not listened to? Or a situation wherein you want to learn a musical instrument and you are told not to

waste your time in useless stuffs and focus on studies instead.
How about a marriage decision wherein the girl or the boy is ***told*** about the marriage and not ***asked***?

Whenever a decision is not mutual and is imposed on the other it gives rise to friction and struggle in relationship. We have to respect and accept independence. The moment you make this magical term the foundation of each of your relationship, you will see the magic happening as I experienced it. And must say I have been blessed by parents who both respect my independence to a great extent. My qualities are just a reflection of what parents gave me. The best gift that parents have given me is the gift of independence and acceptance.

Isn`t it if we base our all our relationships on ***Independence & Acceptance***, rather than expectation, we will have amazing relationships? I will leave that to you to think. Krishna says this is the key to have healthy relationships.

https://www.ramakrishnavivekananda.info/vivekananda/volume_4/lectures_and_discourses/thoughts_on_the_gita.htm

During his sojourn in Calcutta in 1897, Swami Vivekananda used to stay for the most part at the Math, the headquarters of the Ramakrisnna Mission, located then at Alambazar. During this time several young men, who had been preparing themselves for some time previously, gathered round him and took the vows of Brahmacharya and Sannyâsa, and Swamiji began to train them for future work, by holding classes on the Gitâ and Vedanta, and initiating them into the practices of meditation. In one of these classes he talked eloquently in Bengali on the Gita. The following is the translation of the summary of the discourse as it was entered in the Math diary:

Let us see some of the main points discussed in the Gita. Wherein does the originality of the Gita lie which distinguishes it from all preceding scriptures? It is this: Though before its advent, Yoga, Jnana, Bhakti, etc. had each its strong adherents, they all quarrelled among themselves, each claiming superiority for their own chosen path; no one ever tried to seek for reconciliation among these different paths.

It was the author of the Gita who for the first time tried to harmonise these. He took the best from what all the sects then existing had to offer and threaded them in the Gita. But even there Krishna failed to show a complete reconciliation (Samanvaya) among these warring sects, it was fully accomplished by Ramakrishna Paramahamsa in this nineteenth century.

The next is Nishkâma Karma, or work without desire or attachment. People nowadays understand what is meant by this in various ways. Some say what is implied by being unattached is to become purposeless. If that were its real meaning, then heartless brutes and the walls would be the best exponents of the performance of Nishkama Karma. Many others, again, give the example of Janaka, and wish themselves to be equally recognised as past masters in the practice of Nishkama Karma! Janaka (lit. father) did not acquire that distinction by bringing forth children, but these people all want to be

Janakas, with the sole qualification of being the fathers of a brood of children! No!

The true Nishkama Karmi (performer of work without desire) is neither to be like a brute, nor to be inert, nor heartless. He is not Tâmasika but of pure Sattva. His heart is so full of love and sympathy that he can embrace the whole world with his love. The world at large cannot generally comprehend his all-embracing love and sympathy.The reconciliation of the different paths of Dharma, and work without desire or attachment — these are the two special characteristics of the Gita.

Let us now read a little from the second chapter.

सञ्जयउवाच॥

तंतथाकृपयाविष्टमश्रुपूर्णाकुलेक्षणम्।
विषीदन्तमिदंवाक्यमुवाचमधुसूदनः॥१॥

श्रीभगवानुवाच॥

कुतस्त्वाकश्मलमिदंविषमेसमुपस्थितम्।
अनार्यजुष्टमस्वर्ग्यमकीर्तिकरमर्जुन॥२॥

क्लैब्यंमास्मगमःपार्थनैतत्त्वय्युपपद्यते।
क्षुद्रंहृदयदौर्बल्यंत्यक्त्वोत्तिष्ठपरंतप॥३॥

"Sanjaya said:
To him who was thus overwhelmed with pity and sorrowing, and whose eyes were dimmed with tears, Madhusudana spoke these words.

The Blessed Lord said:

In such a strait, whence comes upon thee, O Arjuna, this dejection, un-Aryan-like, disgraceful, and contrary to the attainment of heaven? Yield not to unmanliness, O son of Prithâ! Ill doth it become thee. Cast off this mean faint-heartedness and arise, O scorcher of shine enemies!"

In the Shlokas beginning with तंतथाकृपयाविष्टं, how poetically, how beautifully, has Arjuna's real position been painted! Then Shri Krishna advises Arjuna; and in the words क्लैब्यंमास्मगमःपार्थ etc., why is he goading Arjuna to fight? Because it was not that the disinclination of Arjuna to fight arose out of the overwhelming predominance of pure Sattva Guna; it was all Tamas that brought on this unwillingness. The nature of a man of Sattva Guna is, that he is equally calm in all situations in life — whether it be prosperity or adversity. But Arjuna was afraid, he was overwhelmed with pity. That he had the instinct and the inclination to fight is proved by the simple fact that he came to the battle-field with no other purpose than that.

Frequently in our lives also such things are seen to happen. Many people think they are Sâttvika by nature, but they are really nothing but Tâmasika. Many living in an unclearly way regard themselves as Paramahamsas! Why? Because the Shâstras say that Paramahamsas live like one inert, or mad, or like an unclean spirit. Paramahamsas are compared to children, but here it should be understood that the comparison is one-sided. The Paramahamsa and the child are not one and non-different.

They only appear similar, being the two extreme poles, as it were. One has reached to a state beyond Jnana, and the other has not got even an inkling of Jnana. The quickest and the gentlest vibrations of light are both beyond the reach of our ordinary vision; but in the one it is intense heat, and in the other it may be said to be almost without any heat. So it is with the opposite qualities of Sattva and Tamas.

They seem in some respects to be the same, no doubt, but there is a world of difference between them. The Tamoguna loves very much to array itself in the garb of the Sattva. Here, in Arjuna, the mighty warrior, it has come under the guise of Dayâ (pity).In order to remove this delusion which had overtaken Arjuna, what did the Bhagavân say?

As I always preach that you should not decry a man by calling him a sinner, but that you should draw his attention to the omnipotent power that is in him, in the same way does the Bhagavan speak to Arjuna. नैतत्त्वय्युपपद्यते — "It doth not befit thee!" "Thou art Atman imperishable, beyond all evil. Having forgotten thy real nature, thou hast, by thinking thyself a sinner, as one afflicted with bodily evils and mental grief, thou hast made thyself so — this doth not befit thee!"

— so says the Bhagavan: क्लैब्यंमास्मगमःपार्थ — Yield not to unmanliness, O son of Pritha. There is in the world neither sin nor misery, neither disease nor grief; if there is anything in the world which can be called sin, it is this — 'fear'; know that any work which brings out the latent power in thee is Punya (virtue); and that which makes thy body and mind weak is, verily, sin. Shake off this weakness, this faintheartedness!

क्लैब्यंमास्मगमःपार्थ। —Thou art a hero, a Vira; this is unbecoming of thee."

If you, my sons, can proclaim this message to the world — क्लैब्यंमास्मगमःपार्थनैतत्त्वय्युपपद्यते — then all this disease, grief, sin, and sorrow will vanish from the face of the earth in three days. All these ideas of weakness will be nowhere. Now it is everywhere — this current of the vibration of fear. Reverse the current: bring in the opposite vibration, and behold the magic transformation! Thou art omnipotent — go, go to the mouth of the cannon, fear not.

Hate not the most abject sinner, fool; not to his exterior. Turn thy gaze inward, where resides the Paramâtman. Proclaim to the whole world with trumpet voice, "There is no sin in thee, there is no misery in thee; thou art the reservoir of omnipotent power. Arise, awake, and manifest the Divinity within!"

If one reads this one Shloka — क्लैब्यंमास्मगमःपार्थनैतत्त्वय्युपपद्यते।क्षुद्रंहृदयदौर्बल्यंत्यक्त्वोत्तिष्ठपरंतप॥ — one gets all the merits of reading the entire Gita; for in this one Shloka lies imbedded the whole Message of the Gita.

भावार्थः

इसलिए हे अर्जुन! नपुंसकता को मत प्राप्त हो, तुझमें यह उचित नहीं जान पड़ती। हे परंतप! हृदय की तुच्छ दुर्बलता को त्याग कर युद्ध के लिए खड़ा हो जा॥3॥

Translation

O Parth, it does not befit you to yield to this unmanliness. Give up such petty weakness of heart and arise, O vanquisher of enemies.

Every fool may become a hero at one time or another. Watch a man do his most common actions; those are indeed the things which will tell you the real character of a great man. Great occasions rouse even the lowest of human beings to some kind of greatness, but he alone is the really great man whose character is great always, the same wherever he be.

-Swami Vivekananda

Chapter 7: Meet the Reroes: An Inspirational Dose

Have you come across the term CCTV? Oh! Yes, I am sure you know it.
And now you have already started to think why I suddenly jumped to this irrelevant term.
Let me tell you that you are aware here and now about the term *NOISE*, right? So, **own** your mind here, and stop the *NOISE*. Trust yourselves and you hear the sweet voice form your heart that is never wrong. Always give preference to your heart`s voice and not the *NOISE*.

Let us drive through by applying *HEAL* to our learning now. This time I will do it for you, which will help us sail through our journey in progress.

1. Ok, so who invented CCTV & When?
2. What is the full form of CCTV?
3. How did this idea come into being?

https://reolink.com/cctv-camera-full-form/#what
Let me assist you in finding lesser-known incredible & exciting facts about CCTV cameras here.
The CCTV full form is *closed-circuit television*.
It is a system used to transmit video signals from CCTV cameras to monitors or recorders. It is called " closed-circuit" because the signals are not broadcasted

publicly but are accessed by certain authorized users. Accordingly, the full form of CCTV cameras is closed-circuit television cameras.

Due to the extensive application of CCTV systems in the security industry, CCTV cameras mainly refer to security cameras for home and business surveillance.

Posted by Jonathan Ratcliffe || https://www.cctv.co.uk/when-was-cctv-invented/
The first CCTV system was invented in 1942 during World War Two. Walter Bruch, a German engineer, wanted to be able to monitor V2 rocket launches and hence designed the world's first CCTV system, enabling him to watch the rocket launch from a different location.

However, this was not the full CCTV system as we know it today as there was no way to record a video feed. It was not until 20 years later when Marie Van Brittan Brown in the USA utilized the technology and applied it to a security setting alongside a way of recording footage. This was the world's first CCTV security system, and she and her husband installed the first one in their home. It is thanks to both Walter Bruch and Marie Van Brittan Brown that many of our homes and businesses are protected against burglars by the wonders of CCTV.

(https://economictimes.indiatimes.com/news/politics-and-nation/sales-of-surveillance-cameras-are-soaring-raising-questions-about-privacy-regulation/articleshow/66195866.cms?from=mdr)
According to industry estimates, over a million surveillance units were sold every month a couple of years ago. Now it is two million. The Indian market is growing 20-25% annually, say experts. Industry source

estimate the security & surveillance market was worth Rs 8,200 crore in FY2017, reached Rs 11,000 crore in FY2018,

and is expected to touch Rs 20,000 crore in FY2020. The rise in CCTV coverage can also be observed anecdotally. There's a steady uptick in CCTV clips circulating on Whatsapp, capturing crimes or funny events that would otherwise have gone undocumented. Many of the sensational crimes recently, including multiple incidents of murder in Tamil Nadu, were captured on CCTV cameras, distilling the pure horror of those moments on our mobile screens, and also offering valuable proof to nail the culprits.

Multiple factors are driving the growth in the CCTV segment, says Manu Tiwari, programme manager (automation and electronics practice), Frost and Sullivan. There is a strong governmental push to enhance security; purchases for initiatives such as the Smart City project, which covers 100 cities, and the Rs 2,219 crore allocated under the Nirbhaya Fund for women's safety, which includes eight cities, are some of the growth drivers.
According to Sanjay Kaushik, managing director of security consultancy Nutria Consulting, there is a push to better use CCTV feeds to improve security across India. "While the focus hitherto has been on post facto scouting of footage to find perpetrators, organizations are now trying to be more proactive with their monitoring to spot suspicious people and packages before crimes occur." This could involve closely looking at footage to detect suspicious movements at places such as malls or airports or using technology to spot suspicious objects left unattended for long

periods. Then, there's also a focus on making sure the cameras are installed correctly. "Recognizability is key. Organizations are being pushed to ensure simple things like camera feeds are free of obstructions, license plates are visible in feeds, and there is adequate lighting," adds Kaushik. Advances in technology have ensured that CCTV systems are cheaper and more accessible.

So, after HEALing our information about CCTV, I believe I could put up a few interesting facts.
Moving on from here, what I want to reveal here is a term called CCCTV.

Ok, you think that there is an extra C mentioned. Yes, you caught me red-handed. But, wait, that is not a mistake here. I have deliberately put it here as CCCTV that will help you to sail through the second journey. Do you know who is going to be on board now with us on our journey?

Any guesses?

https://en.wikipedia.org/wiki/G._D._Bakshi

I know this is going to come out from nowhere. And let me onboard and introduce to all of you with immense trust, faith, pride & inspiration, who is a retired Indian army officer. He is from the Jammu and Kashmir Rifles. He was awarded the Vishisht Seva Medal for commanding a battalion in the Kargil War. Later, he was awarded the Sena Medal for distinguished service in commanding a battalion during counter-insurgency drives.

He subsequently commanded the Romeo Force (Part of elite Rashtriya Rifles) during intensive counter-insurgency operations in the Rajouri-Poonch districts of Jammu and Kashmir and succeeded in suppressing the armed militancy in this area. He has served two tenures at the Directorate General of Military Operations and was the first BGS (IW) at HQ Northern Command (India), where he dealt with Information Warfare and Psychological Operations.
He is none other than Major General Gagan Deep Bakshi, aka G. D. Bakshi.

I had my lifetime moment when I could meet him personally at a TEDx event organized by Hansraj College (Delhi University). It was January 18th, 2020, morning, chilled, and foggy weather. It took a lot of courage to bath at 6 AM in the morning to get ready for the workshop as we had to reach sharp at 8:15 AM. Actually, I was surprised when I got to know that such a man is coming. As right from the previous week, I was so engrossed in my daily routine tasks that I could not take the time to read the mail about the event and I could only see a glimpse of the mail that said "All the attendees must reach the venue sharp at 8:15 AM. And I must appreciate the college students and the organizing committee that they were able to nail the event. It was a picture-perfect organization of the event, and I am sure they will do wonders in life.

These are the people that I call the REROES – (Real Heroes). Why a hero should only be "he"? I have a lot of REROES in store for you. So before introducing the heroes of the world who are doing wonders, let me proudly mention few names who work at the ground level tasks and take most of all the pain for the welfare of others.

Three females (whose name I can`t mention of course) besides many hardworking individuals who put their heart and soul to make the event successful. The theme for the event was "Dare to Dream," and yes, these youngsters have dared to dream, and they are already on the path. I could well figure out the real women empowerment rather than in books as most of the team members were female, and I will be wrong if I only call them females. The correct phrase should be FEDERS- (**Fe**male-Lea**ders**), (Feder pronounced as feather). And that's so true to be accurate. They already have their feathers widespread.

The surprising fact here was that my objective to attend the event was to gain some contact as I aspire to be a TEDx speaker so that I could share whatever little I have got with the world. I am still aspiring, or maybe, by the time you board this journey, I may have given a few lectures as a speaker at the TEDx platform. You never know. I can`t explain how badly I want to do this.

And, if I would have given the lectures or short speeches @ TEDx, you may come on board yet another fascinating journey through the videos. So, whether or not I make it, this aspiration landed me up in Hansraj college`s TEDx event.

I learned some of my life-changing lessons from this great man, which I will take you through. Besides this great man, I could also meet some of the fantastic personalities like:

1. ***Yashpal Sharma***, an Indian Bollywood actor, and theatre artist. He is best known for his role as Randhir Singh in Sudhir Mishra's 2003

Hindi movie Hazaaron Khwaishein Aisi, apart from Lagaan (2001), Gangaajal (2003), Ab Tak Chhappan (2004), Apaharan (2005), Singh Is Kinng (2008), Aarakshan (2011) and Rowdy Rathore (2012).

He inspired us to dare to dream, and his aura filled the auditorium with enthusiasm. I was lucky enough to ask him a question on how to have patience while you are on your journey, and the time required demands more patience. He answered it with such ease by sharing his story of his early struggle days.

2. ***Avijit Dutt***, an Indian filmmaker, actor, theater director, and communications consultant. As a Theatre Director & Actor, he has done over 100 plays in English, Hindi & Bengali. He has written 6 full length plays - Bamboo Flower, Mahatma Mar Gaya, Bombay! Bosnia!, Breaking News, Noor Jahan- An Empress Reveals, Unspeakable, 9:45 ki Express ki Citee. He has also dramatized 1084 ki Ma, by Mahasweta Devi, with Shyamanand Jalan. He launched the Childline with UNICEF & National Human Rights Commission.

   Dutt, has played noted roles in Hollywood movies like Kama Sutra: A Tale of Love, Second Best Exotic Marigold Hotel, etc. He has also acted in Madras Cafe as a RAW (Research and Analysis Wing) officer, in Jolly LLB2 as state police head and in No One Killed Jessica as a defense lawyer amongst many. He also inspired us and dared us to dream

3. ***Jeeveshu Ahluwalia,*** whose quick wit can be easily spotted in spontaneous one-liners & quirky jokes. He made his Bollywood debut with "Tamasha," starring Ranbir Kapoor and Deepika Padukone, directed by Imtiaz Ali. His TV Debut was with Zee TV in the comedy show "Gangs of Haseepur." He has been the winner of 'Radio Mirchi Comedy Ka King 2014' and his stand-up videos and comedy sketches have been featured as viral videos on YouTube.

I was so fascinated by his charm, wit, and spontaneity that I gifted him my favorite fountain pen with the words that "I am giving it to you temporarily, and when I will become a Tedx speaker, I will take it back whenever I share the stage with you." I also took his autograph, and he was humble enough so that I could take a snap with him.

So, let me take you through a journey that Retired Major General G.D. Bakshi had taken me through. I could very well connect with his words as it was deeply rooted in my own upbringing. He discussed ***VALUES***, the real *values* that each one of us should have.

He has an astounding personality with the voice close to the roar of a lion.
Let me quickly share with you the *values*.

- C **Country**
- C **Courage**
- C **Compassion**
- T **Truth**
- V **Values**

These values were strongly reinforced during the COVID-19 Pandemic where everyone right from the sweepers to policemen, drivers to sportspersons, small shop owners to big corporate giants, small kids to the superstars of 21st century, nurses to doctors and everyone who have shown that the country is above all. We can well connect to these values very well as we have seen a fresh spell during the outbreak. I would insist you all to pay a close attention to whatever you will read now as this has been lost in the hustle and bustle of life. We as a society somehow have lost connection to these values. We all, including parents, schools, corporates and everyone is responsible for building character of the society. And, if I ask you, what is the character of a society made of? It is made of us. We the people of India. So, let me put forth the values that are my moral, societal and human responsibility.

I would start this by telling you about a painful but yet very deep story. Quickly putting it through. I would like to bring here a small but compelling incident where in members of the Muslim community helped in performing the last rites of their Hindu neighbor in Madhya Pradesh`s Indore city during the quarantine era. The relative of the deceased couldn't reach the place as no vehicle was available due to nationwide lockdown, to carry the body to the cremation ground. Draupadi Bai, a 65-year-old poor woman was suffering from paralysis and died of Covid-19. The Muslim brothers came forward to help the grief-stricken family.

We have a lot of conversation and hatred around Hindu-Muslim tiff, but, isn't this single incident a proof of the values that must be inculcated throughout the society? If this is not an act of value, then what will be?

And one more incident wherein five of our brave soldiers lost their life for saving infiltration activities amid the lockdown and heavy snowfall near the borders. These two and many more endless incidents are living proofs and symbols of such qualities and values. This is it. It is the need of the hour. We must mend our ways and strictly adopt these values and there cannot be a better time than the quarantine era which has provided us with a must needed reset button. Going back to the values

1. **Country:** Needless to say, this was perhaps the first and topmost priority during COVID-19 era. The incidents that I have mentioned and even not mentioned which you all are aware, indicate towards this value of putting your COUNTRY ahead of you. It is the country, and by any means if you ever get a chance to do something for the country, you should feel proud and lucky enough to get this opportunity. Let me take back to the starting line of our journey that said.

"If you ever dreamed of playing for the millions around the world, now is your chance. Play inside, play for the world"

And this was our chance to play for the millions. By staying at home. I would strongly urge everyone right from students to teachers, professionals to businessmen, politicians to bureaucrats, to not indulge in any activity or a contract that by any means has the potential to harm our country. And that is not enough. If you find anyone doing so and if you didn't raise a voice for the fear of losing your job or contracts, even then you are equally harming the society.

This may resemble to the case of Tablighi Jamaat workers, where in with due respect to the Muslim community brothers, they may not have the intention of harming our country by the event, but by concealing the facts and then the hide and seek game played was detrimental. So, if you are not courageous enough to take a stand in favor of our country, then I wonder, of what character and stand you are made of? So, always take a stand for your motherland without the appearance of a drop of fear.

Be a man and woman of character and not the one of mere stand. Whether is it staying at home, or raising voice against the atrocities, be it revealing facts or asking questions for the wrong doings. After all as a son & daughter, would you be able to see your motherland being robbed off her clothes right in front of your eyes? I leave the onus of the answer with you.

2. **Courage:** What can be more courageous to land your life to hell to save others lives? We have so far best examples of the medical staffs, doctors, paramedical staffs, the cleaning staffs besides many others who risked their lives to save ours. Saying thank you looks so tiny and inferior for the efforts they have put in. They risked their life, sacrificed their sleep, and stayed away from their own family members and what not. Their efforts and emotions can`t be simply put in words. I am short of words to praise them from my heart. We are so indebted for their efforts that we can`t pay a return to them.

At least we can do as little as learning from their courageous display of astounding character. Without courage you are just a piece of sand and lack human character. Be it at any level; have courage instilled in your heart. The next question comes, as *what actually it means to be courageous and how to become courageous?* The good news is I have a very simple answer that is derived from the Epic Bhagvad Gita.

Speaking truth without any distortion. If you can tell facts without the influence of situation, you are courageous. If you have the ability to speak what you feel without being affected by the thought of consequences, you are deemed to be courageous. And that's it. It is that simple. And just replace the ability to speak with the ability to act in such situations. And you are the most courageous version of yourself.

3. **Compassion:** I am sure that you must have heard this term before. Let us first understand closely the meaning first. It literally means "to suffer together." Among emotion researchers, it is defined as the feeling that arises when you are confronted with another's suffering and feel motivated to relieve that suffering. So, going by this definition, are you compassionate? Have you ever displayed this trait? I am sure that you have shown this trait knowingly or unknowingly. Can we try to remember any such incident where you felt compassionate enough to help someone in need? Could you feel the pain?

   Do you remember the short story that I mentioned about an old woman whose last rites were performed by our Muslim brothers? Can you connect compassion here?

Yes, that was a pure show of compassion. People moved themselves above the feeling of communities and caste and did what humanity required them to do. Being compassionate is a god gifted character trait and also well developed during the course of character building throughout our lives. Imagine what a great society we will form if this character trait is fostered right form the childhood?

It will set altogether a new dimension to our society. And it was this quality ingrained in all the people who helped amid the pandemic. Be it treating patients, or cleaning hospitals, be it essential food supply or any work that played a role in curbing the deadly situation.

I must bring here the heroics of a 65 year-old person named Arivejagan, from Tamil Nadu. He put a fascinating and compassionate act of courage during the quarantine era. He had a marathon cycling of 130 Km during the lockdown to take his cancer struck wife, Manjula to a hospital. In his amazing act of will power and courage, he made his wife to sit at the back of the bicycle and paddled 18 kms all the way to the hospital just to make sure his wife got treatment at the right time. In this act, he took just two breaks not when he was tired but when his cancer-struck wife was tired sitting for long spells on the bicycle carrier at the back.

During the quarantine era, there were also fake posts. One among such posts was a picture that circulated over social media was Mr.Ratan Tata`s picture on it. Later Mr. Tata revealed that he has not written such a post and if anything he would write, he would better put it on his official website. But to my amazement, the message was strong enough to convince me to bring it here as I loved the message and even if Mr. Tata didn't say it, the message was intact was clear enough to serve its purpose. It gave me a boost in maintaining my own psychological balance. It read as: "Experts are predicting huge down fall of economy due to the Corona." And yes, they are right indeed. But on the other flipside, "we don't know much about these experts. But we know for sure that they don't know anything about the value of human motivation and determined efforts.

If experts were to be believed, after the total destruction in the World War II, Japan had no future. But the same Japan in a matter of just 3 decades or so, made US cry at the market place. If experts were to be believed, Israel should have been wiped out from the world map by the Arabs, but the fact is different. As per the rules of Aerodynamics, the Bumble Bee cannot fly. But it flies as because it doesn't know the rules of aerodynamics. If the experts were to be believed we should have been nowhere in the 1983 world cup. If the experts were to be believed, Wilma Rudolf, the first American Lady to win 4 Olympic Golds in Athletics should not have been in a position to walk without braces, no questions of running. If the experts were to be believed, Arunima Sinha can hardly lead a normal life. But she climbed the Mount Everest.

The Corona crisis in no different, and we don't have doubt about that. We will defeat the Corona virus hands down and the Indian Economy will bounce back in a great manner."

Let us not investigate over the facts or for that matter who has written it. Let us just focus on the essence that these lines are trying to portray. Aren`t these lines meaningful? I leave the question to you to answer.

4. **Truth:** What is truth? Such a stupid question it seems. But let me tell you defining truth a real big deal, isn't it? Can you try to define it? Let us do it then. And I am sure you don't need google to search for the definition.

I will take the help of the Epic ***Bhagvad Gita*** here. *Truth* is defined as *courage*. Saying facts without distortion is truth. Facts put forth as it is. This calls for a very scarce and powerful character trait that we know as *courage*.

But some of you may wonder if we spoke truth all the time, how will we be able to make profits? Or if at all, we tell our bosses that *"I really hate you and your meaningless meetings,"* truth will prove to be fatal, isn't it? Same were the feelings when I first came to know about truth but diving deeper gave me the true picture about ***truth***, and how to execute it in our lives.

To explain this I will bring here a character trait known as ***Honesty***. The challenges associated with honesty are the questions like how much, when and where. Should we be honest even when we know we will incur losses? And I am sure that you have many more like these questions. But I have good news.

The answer lies in the understanding of the term, *honesty*. Let me help you here as a guide.
There are three types of honesty, namely,

i. *Absolute Honesty*

This calls for the situations when you are 100% honest despite the fact that it can be fatal for you or somebody else. And yes, if you thought that it is impractical, you were right indeed. This is not to be followed. And if you have been practicing this for a while to serve the purpose of honesty, you will have to re-think about the definition of honesty. This is destined to always land you into trouble and losses for no reason.

Sometimes you may get fired from your job for giving an honest feedback to your *fixed mindset boss* or you may run into fights and have to suffer for days if you tell *honestly* your wife about the taste of the food that she couldn't make up to your expectation.

And more over if you *honestly* tell your friend that you were able to save, say for example, Rs.50, 000 in last 5 months, you may see your money going to him/her to purchase a new phone from your money. And you are not in a position to demand it when you may need it the most.

So the essence: Don't follow the policy of absolute honesty. It is destined to land you into trouble.

ii. *Calculated Honesty*

This type of honesty is the key to truth. Where you are honest situationally that creates a win-win situation for you as well as others. But let us not confuse this term with diplomacy. To better understand it, let us take an example of visiting a doctor. Even if a patient met an accident and suffered a large cut may be on the back side, the doctor tells that was just a small cut and he will get well soon. And after he is done with his surgery or stitching, he reveals how to take care so that the situation is not taken casual to the extent that it can harm the patient.

A situation where a child of 2 years, while playing with her mom, suddenly falls on a concrete road (just taking the normal fall when a child is learning to walk). She gets up crying aloud like hell. But like most mothers say, "See nothing happened, you are a champ, get up and run again". The child forgets his fall and starts running and this process continues till the child learns how to walk and then run. Consider an office situation wherein a new employee was given a task to do which he couldn't complete up to the mark. But a supervisor praises the hard work he has put in and also tell him how to improve on it.

All the examples mentioned have one central essence and that is ***future benefit***. Calculated honesty demands you not to incur a loss to someone or yourself. If you can practice this, it will open a whole new horizon. I am sure many of you may have been even practicing it. This type of *honesty* also covers all those *lies* that are told not for losses but for the benefit of both the parties, i.e., the speaker as well as the listener.

It demands a lot of courage, empathy and compassion. Imagine if we practice this in the fields of law, science, childcare, and training and where not, the results would be far more than satisfying.

So the essence: Follow the policy of calculated honesty. It is destined to bring you riches.

iii. *Profit-Centric Honesty*

This is perhaps the most dangerous of its kind, where we choose to be honest only for our own profit and benefits. No matter what, we are so cautious about our profits that we ignore the losses that we may incur for others with our honesty. I will strongly advise all not to practice this kind of honesty. In the short term it may fell gratifying but in the longer run, it proves to be fatal.

Say for example, if you are a computer operator working with one of your colleagues. On day he was not feeling well and decided to take a nap on his desk. The moment he puts his head down, your boss entered and you revealed that he was taking a nap and he must not be allowed to do so as it may harm your office culture. You told this with the intention of getting him reprimanded as he was doing a decent job. His firing from your office would have enabled you with more closeness with the boss and you would have become more important to the company.

Your boss in haste, fires him. You started to feel elevated by the feat you have achieved. Soon, a few days later, you realize that work has started to pile up on your shoulders and now you regret your mistake. You also have lost trust of your colleague as well as your boss.

So the essence: Don't follow the policy of profit centric honesty. It is destined to land you into trouble.

5. **Values:** What are the values that define your character? You will have to think deep here before moving on from here. This has the potential to serve the purpose of transforming the way you have been living.

   Do you behave according to your convenience to be saved from a difficult choice or a situation or you still give importance to the values that define your character even if that means a temporary loss or criticism?

   For students, say for example, imagine yourself in a situation wherein the school principle or your class teacher has committed a mistake or has a problem and you want to give him/her a feedback. What would you do in that situation?

For the professionals, let us take an example of a board meeting with all the senior most leaders of the company along with the CEO. The CEO suggests an idea to tackle a problem and every person in the room who are big shots of the company agree with the idea. After all who would endanger their *Sweet Comfy Jobs,* contradicting the CEO? You think the idea is not going to work and you have a better idea.
What would you do in such situation?

Be honest with the answers and that will define the values with which you live by. This outlines your character which in turn expresses your overall persona and self-respect.

Let me make it simpler by revealing my values which in turn define my character and every day decisions.

So I delve on the below mentioned values:

1. **Impacting Lives**
2. **Empowering People**
3. **Creating win – win situation**

I follow a formula of 3 * 3 wherein for each of the above mentioned values I have adopted 3 ways that are well defined.

For the first one, **impacting lives**, I religiously write books, give training sessions & assist people with my social work projects of education, providing food and clothes etc. These three actions in some way or the other help me in fulfilling my first value.

For the second one, **empowering people**, I always bestow my team members with responsibilities that they can handle, I include team members in the decision making process and teach one new thing each day.

For the third one, creating **win-win situation,** I always try to make sure that I provide value first when I am seeking services from someone, get to learn one thing from a person with whom I work, gift or highlight one positive trait that he/she has on which he/she can further work.

Can I ask you diligently, to form a ***formula of 3 * 3*** in your daily lives? I have been practicing it for more than 5 years and the results have been far more than fabulous. So I urge you to write down 3 values for yourselves that define your character and further 3 ways for each of the value to support them.

When you retire every day from your schedule you can take a daily inventory of how much have you contributed to values. These three values should be such that it defines your character and people recognize you for these values. Remember that saying of, ***"People always remember, how you made them feel."*** Defining these values help you to exactly do this.

You should practice this daily and if you do so, you will soon see wonders happening in your professional and personal lives. So before accelerating further I would urge all of you to first define your personal ***3 * 3 formula***. Your daily actions should be supporting these values. This will give you a whole new perspective towards working and maintain your strong character and growth.

Going back to the examples of scenarios that I have put in, you will stand by your values and tell your principal politely maintaining the dignity of his/her position about the feedback.

For the second example, again without offending your company`s CEO, you will present your idea and tell honestly how you feel about his idea. And, the CEO of a ***growth mindset*** will be more than happy with your stand. And if at all, the CEO is of a ***fixed mindset***, he will give indication of arrogance and would be offended. This single incident is enough to update your resumes and look out for opportunities waiting for you. And if this is the reason for your job change, it is worth the change. Praise yourself that you are courageous enough to speak. You may suffer temporary crisis of misbehavior or sniffs from your seniors but remember in the longer run, it is only you whom you have to report to.

Do take some time out to define this formula for you. It is so gratifying and uplifting.

Going back to the title of the chapter i.e. *Meet the Reroes: An inspirational dose*, where the term *Reroes* refers to **Re**al life her**oes**, we already have so many heroes from almost every spheres of the society. We have seen how Shri Aditya Nath Yogi, sacrificed his presence in his father`s last rites. How police personnel despite being stone pelted continued to serve for the mankind. Many of them also got infected and few of them lost their lives in the battle. Kids who donated their piggy bank savings. Police officers who even cooked and made masks for distribution. Medical staffs who untiringly continued to hover around the contaminated zones to save lives. The Paralympians who made our country proud.

Many of them also sacrificed their lives. Muslim brothers performing the last rites of a Hindu old woman in Indore. The list is endless it will go on and on. These are the real heroes who must be praised whole heartedly and not only praising will help but to take their legacy forward will be the biggest praise for them and for the generations to come. I hope not to see such a calamitous situation in our country again but better be prepared and strengthen our roots.

But the thing to notice here that to be a real life hero, it requires values ingrained in our heart and whenever our country requires, we should be ready with a smile to defeat anyone and anywhere, be it the COVID-19 Pandemic or terrorists, hunger or the essentials-Illiteracy or poor health, racism and differentiation on the basis of caste, creed, sex or religion. These all are our enemies and to fight such deep rooted opponents we need to pull our socks up. You don't need to be qualified as a hero to put your best foot forward. You just need to *qualify as a human* that is fairly possible by developing these qualities. The Pandemic has been a harsh yet effective teacher to take us back to our roots which had diminished with due course of time.

I would urge all the educators and those responsible in the immaculate professions of teaching, leading and others to strengthen these qualities in themselves and to pass on the legacy to the younger generations.

Schools, colleges and corporates all have to work in unison to develop these values of **CCCTV.**

"We have succeeded to make the phones smart, and in return the smartphones have succeeded to make us not so smart.

Chapter 8: Relationship with Technology & Digital Dementia

Reference: Spitzer M. (2012). Digitale demenz
https://www.psychologytoday.com/intl/blog/mind-change/201507/digital-dementia
https://www.psychologytoday.com/intl/blog/mind-change/201504/iphone-therefore-i-am
https://blog.designsforhealth.com/digital-dementia
https://elearningindustry.com/8-second-attention-span-organizational-learning
https://www.sycamorevalleychiropractic.com/digital-dementia-a-modern-day-health-epidemic/
https://www.chieflearningofficer.com/2018/03/02/conquering-attention-residue/

Barr, N., Pennycook, G., Stolz, J. A., & Fugelsang, J. A. (2015). The brain in your pocket: Evidence that Smartphones are used to supplant thinking. Computers in Human Behavior
De Neys, W., & Glumicic, T. (2008). Conflict monitoring in dual process theories of thinking. Cognition.

Has the time come to redefine our relationships with technology? Has our relationship with technology taken over other relationships with *life* and other significant realities?

Let us *scroll* through few facts that will help us to understand is there any need to redefine our relationship with the virtual reality.

You have read in earlier chapters about mind and its functions. I assume that we all have at least fair knowledge about it if not the complete knowledge. I also want to be clear that I am in no way against the use of technology. I am myself a big supporter, promoter and adopter of technology. But the onus lies in defining our *marriage rules* with it.

Let us start with the term ***Digital Dementia***. Have you heard it before? If not, I will make it easy for you. The best example of this term can be routed to a day when on 3rd March 2020, India`s PM Shri Narendra Modi tweeted about leaving social media. He also realized something that he could go to the extent of denouncing social media usage.

Digital Dementia is a term devised by neuroscientist Dr. Manfred Spitzer, German neuroscientist and psychiatrist. It can be best described as overuse of digital technology that results in the collapse of cognitive abilities (like logical and reasoning, thinking, short and long term memory, attention, visual processing etc.). Spitzer explains that short-term memory pathways will start to deteriorate from underuse if we overuse technology. In 2012 Spitzer was concerned about the rising number of children and adults with memory and cognitive problems. He also published a book titled *Digital Dementia: What We and Our Children are Doing to our Minds.*

Let me give you a real life scenario. I was sitting with my trainees at a restaurant enjoying a delightful meal as a deserved award for successfully completing a training batch. The training had lasted for a period of around 10 days of grueling facts, understanding, website exploration of the client, fact sheets and much more. So on the final day after successful results we decided to give ourselves a treat. We were a total of 10 including me. As soon as we finished the brunch the bill was handed over to us by the waiter. The bill amounted to Rs. 1240. This bill was to be split between 10 people. So one of my trainees took out his smart phone, opened the calculator and with immense proud of being the quickest one to tell us, he informed us that each one of us has to pay Rs. 124. All sounds good here. I asked him that it doesn't sound correct. So, now everyone to prove their intelligence took out their smart phones in haste and arrived at the answer yelling Rs.124 as the correct split. What`s wrong here?

I told them that I am still was not convinced. So I called the waiter. I asked him to split the bill of Rs.1240 among 10, and tell how much each of us owes to the restaurant. Without thinking for even half of a second he exclaimed!! "Rs. 124 Sir".

Now I agreed that this time it was correct. Let us pay and move out. So we paid our shares and moved out. Later on, my trainees asked me what was wrong with you Sir. We had told you the same amount as the waiter told you and not only once but twice. I answered did you notice the process how he arrived at the answer and how you all did the same thing.

Can you get the essence now? For such a small task to divide by 10, do we really need to use a calculator?

Do we really need a smart phone to decide on as small things as these?

Have we *outsourced* our cognitive skills like memory to smart phones? Our brains strictly obey one policy i.e., ***use it or lose it***. Without the regular practice of using, storing and retrieving facts, our ability to do has diminished and risks being further diminished.

The above incident at the restaurant calls for a term ***cognitive miserliness***. It means that today we are unwilling to invest cognitive energy to solve the problem by simply thinking about it. "Those who use their smart phones and computers and Google simple questions actually know the answer or could easily learn it." This is proposed by researchers where in a series of three studies on US workers and Canadian college students, cognitive miserliness was measured with questions such as these:

In a study 1000 people were tested. Among the participants there were 3 who live in a condo and 997 who live in a farmhouse. Kurt is a randomly chosen participant of this study. Kurt works on Wall Street and is single. He works long hours and wears Armani suits to work. He likes wearing sunglasses.

What is most likely?

A. Kurt lives in a condo
B. Kurt lives in a farmhouse

In questions such as these, an individual who is prone to high levels of cognitive miserliness will choose to answer quickly and intuitively to select A, and use their analytical, resource-intensive thought process to arrive at the correct answer B.

Researchers further found that there has been increased reluctance to spend energy on thinking. If we use smartphone, computers and technology to *connect the dots*, then our ability to make new connections- to convert information to knowledge and then knowledge to action-may also is in difficulty.

South Korea has fronted the research into digital dementia. Dr. Byun Gi-Wun a South Korean expert in cognitive problems is concerned that "heavy reliance on smartphones creates an imbalance in brain development which leads to the left side of the brain becoming overstimulated while the right side suffers and becomes relatively stunted. Heavy use of smartphones engages the left brain at the expense of the right leading to deterioration of right side-leaning cognitive abilities and symptoms of 'digital dementia' which include loss of memory, short attention span and problems regulating emotion."

Currently a large cohort study that seeks to investigate an association between technology use in secondary education children and cognitive or behavioral development is in progress. Study of Cognition and Mobile Phone (SCAMP) will be the largest study in the world to address the issue of technology and cognition. This research will be led by Department of Epidemiology and Biostatistics at Imperial College London in collaboration with Birkbeck, University of London, and the Swiss Tropical Public Health Institute .This study is focusing its attention on the potential impact of electromagnetic radiation on language understanding attention planning and memory. The results could provide yet another reason for the rise in digital dementia among those with frequent use of digital technology.

You can measure qualitatively whether you are under some influence of this phenomenon of dementia. How? I am giving you a very simple way to gauge.

Just try counting the number of times you have used your smartphone while reading this book. And if you want to be more precise quantitatively, set a time of book reading for 1 or 2 hours. During this time also keep a blank paper in which you will tick mark every time you pick up your gadget. Also tick mark the number of times you crave for your smartphone. A higher number of cravings would represent a significant influence of dementia. I am sure you will be surprised to know about the craving for your smart phone.

I am yet to give a number below which you are safe and an optimum and danger mark. May be in later and revised editions of the book you may be able to figure out this number.

You may have encountered the famous and glorified infographic about attention span at 12 seconds in the year 2000 and 8 seconds in 2013. It also cited attention span of Goldfish as 9 seconds. Where do these numbers come from? And can they help us in improving our attention?

The answer to the first question, the numbers appear to be fiction cited by advertisers to catch the eyeballs. The source can neither be traced to National Center for Biotechnology Information, U.S. National Library of

Medicine, The Associated Press nor other legitimate sources.

The answer to the second question, of whether these numbers can help us in our attention or not, a better help would be to understand what is attention and its types. Here I will also try to help you with actions that can help to increase cognitive skills.

Let us understand types of attention through Sohlberg and Mateer's Attention Model, which was developed for clinical use but can be of good help for us too.

Levels	Description
1. Focussed Attention(Easiest Level)	Response to External Stimuli. Example: Reacting when touched
2. Sustained Attention	Ongoing focus to carry out repetitive tasks. Example: Remembering instructions and carrying them out when needed
3. Selective Attention	Staying focussed while distractions are present. Example: Reading a book while travelling in a metro
4. Alternating Attention	Shifting focus between tasks that need different skills. Example: Alternating between asking questions, listening for answers and typing in facts on a form.
5. Divided Attention (Most difficult Level)	Responding simultaneously to multiple tasks Example: Talking on the phone while sending emails

Table 1. Sohlberg and Mateer Attention Model (adapted from Sohlberg & Mateer reference)

We all can find ourselves in one or multiple levels. In addition to the model above, Chun, Golumb, and Turk-Browne further describes 2 types of attention

1. **External:** It refers to all the selections of external information and processing through our senses from the world.

2. **Internal:** It refers to the process of selecting and processing information from pre-existing facts, memories, attention etc. internally. We access here the already existing information with us.

The learning process involves both the type of attention and an understanding of both the types of attention coupled with the model above can help us to be more precise and efficient in while learning.
The above understanding can also help organizations design and provide a conducive environment depending on the attention level a work demands.

Attention residue, as explained by Sophie Leroy, an assistant professor in the UW Bothell School of Business, is "when thoughts about a task persist and intrude while performing another task. Those lingering thoughts use up important cognitive processing power that can't be devoted to the new task.
Individuals burdened with attention residue are essentially "functioning with a reduced cognitive capacity." Switching frequently between tasks and allowing more unmanaged interruptions can have a huge impact on performance. The transition has to be guided to one. And multitasking is now an old-fashioned verb.

The discussion above suggests that, at first we have to accept that technology has impacted our learning process so we must teach especially the younger generation accordingly and differently. We have to define our relationship with the technology and also help the younger generations establish healthier relationships with the tech world. It is not a calling for a complete ***divorce*** with technology but rather re-established *marriage* with defined independence and dependence.

It is not about how many seconds and minutes one can focus, but how not to allow technology adversely affect our cognitive abilities that set us apart.

Let us now scroll through some major problems we all are facing especially youngsters.
The signs of digital dementia can range from short-term memory loss, anxiety, depression, and anger, lower acceptance of feedback to slouched posture, minimal or no movement and social seclusion. Before going to the solutions of digital dementia, it will be worth to understand how it develops. Perhaps a simpler answer would be overuse of technology and being dependent on it for even simple tasks.

We should also know a more detailed answer. It occurs when individuals spend an excessive amount of time on their gadgets with poor posture a sensory dissociation occurs at the back of the brain which is overactive and the front of the brain which is under active.

As you have read fairly about different lobes of brain, especially the frontal lobe, it will be easy to relate here. In case needed, you must refer the chapter, *Inside the mind*. The occipital lobe in the back of the brain processes visual signals such as visual cues from a video game, social media or TV program. While seated and engaged with technology, the front part of the brain including the frontal and parietal lobes, are under-stimulated. These regions of the brain are responsible for higher order thinking and good behaviors such as motivation, goal setting, reading, writing, memory and socially appropriate behaviors. These areas of the brain are also responsible for movement and body position sense.

With the paragraph above you may well understand what actually happens inside the brain that leads to digital dementia.

Next question we should ask- Is there any way to stay away from digital dementia? What are the steps we can take to increase our cognitive skills? The good news is we have answers to both the questions.

Technology is ubiquitous and we cannot and should not dump technology. How we engage with technology and redefine our relationship with it can help us amazingly to curb digital dementia and make the most of our powerful brains.

The first one you have already gone through in the section of earlier chapters, *Mind and exercise*. Here we will look especially with respect to dementia.

1. ***Dance your brain out:*** Yeah!! You heard it right. Dance your brain out means keeping a significant amount of time (a minimum of 30 Min to 60 Minutes) for few activities like:

a) *Scribing/Writing, memorizing favorite songs or dance steps.*
b) *Playing chess or other mind engaging games.*
c) *Reading a book, during a break, before bedtime or anytime you can.*

2. ***Increase play time while reducing the screen time***: This holds true not just for youngsters and teenagers but also to adults. By play time I mean, especially outdoors. It activates our sensory and motor cortex from movement and physical sensation. This may sound obvious but it has scientific reasons. As you are running around, jumping up and down and swinging back and forth, you are developing fine motor pathways and are stimulating the part of your brain to improve your balance and posture. "Play" is of vital importance to the development of children and for the maintenance of health of adults and the elderly.

3. ***Your spine is responsible for the stimulation and nutrition of your brain:*** Make sure you take good care of your spine so that it takes care of your brain. This can easily be done by maintaining good posture. Not using compromising posture while working and using laptop.

4. ***Reduce Stress:*** Do anything that makes you laugh enjoy but healthier ones. Don't indulge into habits of drinking and intoxication to feel good

5. **Care for your body:** Not very difficult though we have made it a bit hyped. Drink enough water, at least 7 hours of sleep, physical and mental exercise 3 to four times a week for 36-60 minutes and a balanced diet is all it takes to care for your body. Just count 5 4 3 2 1 and go! No need to set targets and make hyped plans. It is your duty towards your gifted body.

6. **Practice focusing:** Just find a quiet place and focus on breathing. Or else put your ear pods on with some nice soothing flute music and give your mind a peaceful time. That's it! No need to worry about the technicalities. Just start now!

Chapter 9: HOTS: *High Opportune Trainable Skills*, which are rarely taught.

- Self-Regulation
- Top 5 Languages of the world:
- Motivation
- 56 Deltas, across 13 skills groups & 4 Categories

Under this section, I have tried to cover as it is obvious from the title of the chapter. As a learner, trainer and a CBT practitioner I find these skills a must need for students, parents, teachers and professionals. It needs a place in educational institutions and is our responsibility as well to inscribe these skills in early stages of learning and development of an individual. After going through unending experiential learning, I have found these to play a pivotal role to confront major challenges of the modern lives.

Gone are the days of learning just limited to text book and century old method of learning & development? It is time to get ourselves updated with actionable life skills. Let us not tag these skills with life transformation and other mental healing processes. Rather these skills present us all with a new beginning towards the cognitive process of learning.

1. *Self-Regulation:*

Let us start this from a recent news in `The Economic times` daily newspaper dated 29th May 2020, Friday. In one of the sections it said that a new model is being proposed for Indian Educational System. The normal 220 hours yearly learning at school to be split in to three parts of 100, 100 and 20 hours respectively. The first hundred hours is to be dedicated to normal brick and mortar structure of in-school learning. The next 100 hours for `active self-learning` at home. And the remaining 20 hours, the major area of interest, to be used for emotional well-being of students. If these 20 hours can be focused on and efficiently utilized and implemented, it can complement the remaining 200 hours more than anything.

Cutting long story short, this step clearly shows that we now have gradually realized the importance of emotional well-being of students that can be taken care only by specialists in this field ranging from counselors, CBT practitioners, psychologists and others of the same genre. This drills down to ***self-regulating skills*** that I want to bring here. It is certainly one of the skills that are rarely taught and considered at educational institutions, and qualifies to be classified into our list of HOTS.

As a Cognitive Behavior Therapist (CBT practitioner), I see an immense potential and at the same time a major need for self-regulation right from the early stages of growth. It has the potential to solve a lot of problems that arise in a human`s life time. It can help to tackle problems in relationships, studies, stress management, people management besides a crucial list of many other problems.

Jean Piaget, a Swiss Psychologist, known for his work on child`s development says: *"The main goal of education should be to create mature adults who are confident in learning how to solve problems for themselves instead of repeating what other generations have done before them"*. This stands so true to be true.

Let us first understand clearly what self-regulation is and how we can develop these skills. We will also explore the areas of life that it can be implemented on. You will be surprised to know how efficient and easy it is to apply the skill. You will find this as a major miss in our educational system.

https://positivepsychology.com/self-regulation/
Consider any of the following situation(s) for an insightful understanding:

1. Can you think of a recent incident where you muddled with your parents for not allowing the freedom you need?
2. Can you think of a recent incident when you were driving or riding a bike and suddenly a car zoomed past your vehicle and you abused the driver of the car like anything?
3. During the recent spell of the COVID-19, did you allow it to affect your sleeping and eating habits?
4. Can you think of an incident when your boss took it really bad on you and scolded you for your mistakes and later on, when you left the discussion thought him as one of the worst human in your life?

Let us explore each of the situations one at a time and try to understand the difference between a self-regulated behavior and a behavior that is on the flipside.

Firstly, when muddling with your parents over an issue to go out with your close friends, ***a self-regulated behavior*** would mean that you choose not to argue with them and let them have the final say. You waited for them to calm down and then choose the sweet spot of time to restart the discussion which can potentially let you win the permission.

On the flipside, if you choose to argue over and play tantrums if they denied you the permission, you also closed the door for a healthy discussion later on at the sweet spots. Where can you fit yourselves here honestly?

In the second situation, when you were driving, did you choose to abuse the driver who zoomed past you or did you think that he/she might be in emergency that made him/her to drive that way. What a contrasting way of thinking! And imagine the tremendous effect it has on your mood. It hardly takes seconds to regulate but has an impressive long term effect on our ability.

2. ***Top 5 Languages of the world: The E4L***

   The Language of experience
   The Language of emotions
   The Language of empathy
   The Language of smile
   The Language of love

3. *Motivation*

How do you motivate yourselves? Do you really need a person to motivate you? If these are recurring questions for you, let me put it another way.

I am sure we all agree that it is a must have for everyone. I will not take you to the theories of motivation. I just want to share here what I have understood through my experiential learning.
I have encountered.

Apart from these I would like to highlight few skills that are must to survive and excel now and in future. We may discuss these mutually on the lines of:

A. Why are these important?
B. What are these skills?
C. How can we acquire these skills?

As I have to restrict myself to adhere to timelines and to stop myself from scribing otherwise I will keep on writing and the book will never come into being. But still you take the most of it.

Feel free to connect to know more about these skills and effective ways to acquire.

Reach me @ :
https://www.linkedin.com/company/the-journey-to-a-new-you
https://www.facebook.com/simpliiawesome
https://www.instagram.com/rahul.thakurkp/

According to a latest research by McKinsey & Company, below are the areas where we need to have a niche if we want to foster sustainably.

"Talk to yourself at least once in a day. Otherwise, you may miss a meeting with an excellent person in this world."

—Swami Vivekananda

The Final Destination: Meet your someone special.

So here we come to meet a fantastic person. Yes, he or she is right there with you inside you. You can observe yourselves and have a checkup from the neck up to see the changes and how it has been to sail through the path of

THE JOURNEY TO A NEW YOU...

ABOUT THE AUTHOR:

"I am a good reader that helps me to grow;
I am a good musician that helps me to throw.
I am a learner that helps me to bow;
I am a helper who helps you to know;
I am a sportsperson who helps you to **get set go**...."

-By the Author

The Author defines himself as an "Enabler". So true to be true. Struggling in his initial years in childhood with a variety of interests and hobbies, his parents even said that he is not able to focus on one thing and still some tiny dialogues keep coming from his parents.

But after meeting the real world of possibilities and plethora of opportunities, all thanks to his various interests in the field of education, sports, music. He believes that "art" brings people together. "You don't need to do much to help each other. You just need to have good intentions."

With his creative pursuits and human approach, he is a brutal and lethal reader + writer + public speaker, a cricket & badminton geek, swimming fan, a carefree traveler, a guitar person along with fair vocal skills. Recently he has picked up 10m Air rifle and pistol shooting which he is currently loving. He is quite good at making sketch and portraits. He loves to make power point presentations. He is a huge server of nature and spends most of his time in nature meditating along the way to his work.

People are amazed to see how he is able to find such laps of nature. He is an amazing person to talk to as he always finds time to talk to you. The best subject that he likes to study is *Human*. And he loves to interact with known and unknown people to learn from them while also sharing his knowledge. He is a huge seeker of knowledge and forever hungry and thirsty for it. He embraces the idea of how our mind works and keeps on inventing the ways to use the brain to maximum.

Even if you watch his video series like *"CAREERINA"*- that aims to help everyone on personal + professional development &*"FEDERs"* – that aims towards women empowerment in the field of education, health and societal challenges through power conversation with FEmale leaDERS, you will always see a dose of nature along with great insights.

"What do you want to be when you grow up?"
This question has been surrounding his entire childhood, and you also may very well resonate with this question. He didn't have the answer as he couldn't tell 20 different things that he likes and want to be.

But he was quick enough to realize in his early teens that he is a **MULTIPOTENTIALITE**, and there is nothing wrong in having varied interests. This is not a limitation or a weakness according to him, this virtue is his strength and sets him apart. He defines his strengths as:

1. **Idea Synthesis**
2. **Rapid learning**
3. **Never shying away from trying something new**

He is a Post-Graduate with MBA in HR from All India Management association and also possesses a Masters in Data Science from Purdue University. He is also a CBT (Cognitive Behavioral Therapist) Practitioner certified from The Academy of Modern Applied Psychology. He carries with himself 15 + 8 Years of Experience. Fifteen years of initial learning and eight years of professional experience. Currently, at the time of writing, he heads the training and recruitment department of an Indo-Spanish MNC.He emphasizes importance to those early fifteen years that paved the way for the next 8 years. He restricts himself from boasting about his achievements. Practicing humility & modesty, when he is asked about his achievements, he exclaims that the greatest achievement he has ever earned is "Knowing himself" and taking care of his parents. Rest of the achievements he considers as temporary with a timeline that will fade away. He wishes everyone good luck and the courage to conquer whatever challenge may come across with a growth mindset and *feeding* wolf of courage instead of feeding wolf of fear`. (Here Wolf=mind)

https://www.linettebixby.com/post/i-asked-the-leaf

I asked the leaf whether it was frightened because it was autumn and the other leaves were falling. The leaf told me, "No. During the whole spring and summer I was completely alive. I worked hard to help nourish the tree, and now much of me is in the tree. I am not limited by this form. I am also the whole tree, and when I go back to the soil, I will continue to nourish the tree. So I don't worry at all.

As I leave this branch and float to the ground, I will wave to the tree and tell her, 'I will see you again very soon.' "That day there was a wind blowing and, after a while, I saw the leaf leave the branch and float down to the soil, dancing joyfully, because as it floated it saw itself already there in the tree. It was so happy. I bowed my head, knowing that I have a lot to learn from the leaf.

- **Thich Nhat Hanh**

Printed by Libri Plureos GmbH in Hamburg,
Germany

9 789354 723735